Analysis of Performance for GCSE PE

Julie Walmsley

ACKNOWLEDGEMENTS

The publishers would like to thank the following for permission to reproduce photographs:

Actionplus on pp. 18, 19, 30b, 35, 72, 79, 116b

De Vere Group/Greens Health and Fitness on p.55

Digitial Vision on p.33

EMPICS on pp. 12, 15, 21, 22, 30a, 37, 59, 60, 62, 63, 64, 80, 104, 105, 109, 110, 111, 114, 115, 116a

Getty Images on pp. 36, 40, 57

John Birdsall Photo Library on p.118

Mark Shearman Sports Photography on p.39

PhotoDisc on pp. 20, 42,

Stockbyte on pp. 124, 125

SWpix on pp. 32, 81, 83, 99, 100, 101, 113

UK: Folens Publishers, Apex Business Centre, Boscombe Road, Dunstable, LU5 4RL.
Email: folens@folens.com

Ireland: Folens Publishers, Greenhills Road, Tallaght, Dublin 24.
Email: info@folens.ie

Poland: JUKA, ul. Renesansowa 38, Warsaw 01-905.

Editor: Caroline Marmo

Text design and layout: Pumpkin House, Cambridge

Illustrations: Mark Stacey

Cover design: Martin Cross

Cover image: © Jon Feingersh/CORBIS

First published 2004 by Folens Limited.

British Library Cataloguing in Publication Data. A catalogue record for this publication is available from the British Library.

ISBN 1-84303-629-0

CONTENTS

INTRODUCTION

This book will support the areas of study and skill required in the eleven key topics listed in the matrix below. Its aim is to provide information not only for the analysis of performance section, but also on officiating, the different roles within sport and how leadership influences the sportsperson.

TOPIC	PAGES	EDEXCEL	AQA	OCR
1 Officiating	6–16	Criteria 1	Skill Area C	A01
2 Appreciating the role of rules	17–20	Criteria 1	Skill Area C	A01
3 Using the correct terminology	21–25	Criteria 1	Skill Area C	A01
4 Observation and analysis	26–33	Criteria 2	Skill Area D	A02
5 Recognising strengths and weaknesses	34–101	Criteria 3	Skill Area D	A02
6 Applyng knowledge, principles, methods and training practices	50–59 72–80 94–101	Criteria 4	Skill Area D	A02
7 Setting targets	105–108	Criteria 4	Skill Area D	A02
8 Monitoring	108–109	Criteria 4	Skill Area D	A02
9 Using PEP	56–58 78–79 99–100	Criteria 4	Skill Area D	A02
10 Understanding leadership	109–111	Criteria 5	N/A	N/A
11 Different roles in the activity	112–116	N/A	Skill Area E	N/A
% of total final marks		**10%**	**18%**	**10%**

A01 = Assessment Objective 1   A02 = Assessment Objective 2

1 ► CHOOSING YOUR SPORT TO ANALYSE

Throughout your PE GCSE, you will be asked to build up your skills of analysis, observation and officiating. In order to do this, you must gain as much experience from the practical lessons as possible. Take the opportunity to analyse and officiate whenever you can. For the examination, you will have to name the sport you are analysing; so you must familiarise yourself with that sport as much as possible.

Factors affecting your choice may be:

- Is it your favourite sport?
- Is it your best performance sport?
- Is it the sport you know most about?
- Is it a sport with lots of information readily available?
- Is it a sport with simple tactics and basic skills, which are easy to understand and analyse?
- Is it a sport where you have access to all the necessary equipment and facilities?

For the purpose of this book we have chosen to include examples of both static and dynamic stretching. However, please check current research and ask your teacher about their preferred stretching techniques before undertaking any warm-up or cool down exercises.

2 ► PREPARATION FOR SUCCESSFUL ANALYSIS

Use this list to guide you through the skills necessary for success:

- know your sport
- know the perfect model for your chosen technique
- be able to use the correct terminology
- know the tactics (basic – intermediate – advanced)
- gain experience from watching and reading about your chosen sport
- join in class discussions – this will gradually increase your confidence in expressing your thoughts
- make sure you have umpired/refereed or judged your sport so that you are confident with the rules, regulations and procedures
- practise analysing your activity, and save the results for reference and revision
- practise recording a performance so that each time you do it, you can concentrate more on the action.

1 OFFICIATING

This section contains:

1. ▸ Rules make the game
2. ▸ Referees and umpires
3. ▸ Skills of the referee and umpire
4. ▸ Duties of a referee/umpire
5. ▸ An umpire's actions at an infringement
6. ▸ How to improve your knowledge
7. ▸ How to build up umpiring experience
8. ▸ Judging a competition

There are several aspects to the officiating section of the examination. These range from the type of officials in a sport, to the rules they keep, and why and how they keep them in a game situation. To be able to officiate well takes study and practice, so take every opportunity to organise, coach, referee and umpire. Start with a small group, perhaps of younger players, and gradually build up your confidence.

1 ▸ RULES MAKE THE GAME

Every game is different due to the rules and regulations influencing the play. These rules and regulations not only give the sport its individuality, but also provide a basis for fair play between the teams or players and keep injuries to a minimum.

Rules determine how games are played and the competition is won – is a goal scored or a missile placed where it cannot be reached? The size of the teams, duration of play and the dimensions of the pitch are all stipulated in the rules of a game.

Each game or sport has its own rules on fouling. In basketball, for instance, players are allowed to foul four times, but on the fifth foul they are disqualified from play. Therefore, during the game, players use the fouls system for the benefit of the team. This is a recognised tactic of basketball, and is not seen as 'dirty' play. In most other sports and games this system of specific fouls does not exist. Players rely on the discretion of the referee or umpire to discipline infringements of the rules. Sometimes, however, spectators can see the subjective view of the official as the rules are applied inconsistently.

2 ▸ REFEREES AND UMPIRES

There are various officials linked with all sports. Some activities need only a few people to run the game, whereas others need more due to the complexity of the game. A basketball game can include the following officials, all necessary for the smooth running of a match:

**Referee   Umpire   Commissioner   Scorer
Assistant scorer   Timekeeper   24-second operator**

The most common official in sport is the referee or umpire. It is their job to make sure that teams or players keep to the rules and ensure there is no unfair advantage. Good officials will oversee games with confidence and efficiency. They are unable to improve a match but, on some occasions, a bad referee can spoil a game.

Although there is often more than one official at a game, there will be normally only one official who has overall responsibility. A good example of this is in the game of rounders. Let's look at this in more detail.

There are two umpires, who have joint responsibility for clearly announcing the decisions and scores, checking the pitch, equipment, players' clothing and keeping records of the score and batters out. Each umpire can dismiss players from the pitch for unsporting conduct. As well as these dual responsibilities, each umpire has a specific role to play and a position to adopt during the game.

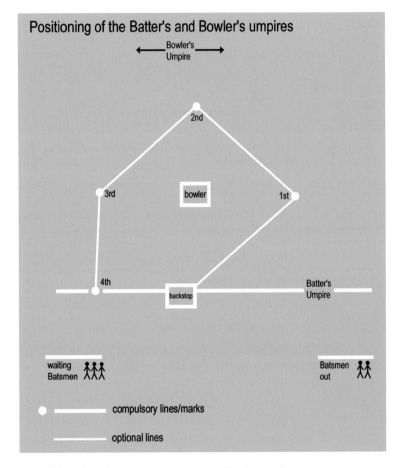

▲ *Position of the batter's and bowler's umpires in rounders.*

The batter's umpire

- stands at the end of the batting line, so they can see the first post easily
- calls 'no-ball' if the bowler's action is not continuous, if the bowler bowls with a foot over the front line of the bowling square, if the ball passes above the head or below the knee of the batter or for any bowl that hits the ground before reaching the batter

- calls 'rounder' or 'half rounder' when they are scored
- gives any decisions concerning the front line or back line of the batting square
- gives decisions on 'backward hits' and calls them when necessary
- gives decisions on the first and fourth posts
- gives decisions on all catches
- calls the next player (by name or number) to the batting square.

The bowler's umpire

- stands behind and away and to the right of the third post so they can see the pitch
- calls 'play' at the beginning of each innings
- calls 'play' to restart the game after a dead-ball situation
- calls 'no-ball' for wide bowls, balls that hit or would have hit the player if they had not moved or bowls passing on the non-hitting side of the batter
- gives decisions on the second and third posts
- calls 'no-ball' if the bowler's foot goes over the back line or side line of the bowling square
- ensures the waiting batters and those batters that are out stay behind their relevant lines.

So we can see from this short look at the two umpires in rounders, that it is important to know what your responsibilities are in the game, so you know when, and what, to call. Your chosen sport will have direct guidelines as to each official's responsibilities in its rule book.

To be a good official or referee takes time, practice and experience. The referees and umpires we see on television have worked hard to reach that standard. They have passed examinations, attended courses and kept up to date with developments in umpiring and refereeing in their sport to be the best they can.

Referees need a thorough knowledge and understanding of the rules and how they are applied in a game before beginning to referee. This allows them to use the correct terminology and hand signals when controlling the game. With practice and experience they gradually become more confident and efficient in applying rules appropriately.

3 ▸ SKILLS OF THE REFEREE AND UMPIRE

There are certain skills a referee or umpire should have in order to do their job well:

a) Concentration

b) Movement and positioning

c) Observation

d) Communication.

a) Concentration

- focus on the job of officiating
- refrain from being distracted from people outside the match
- maintain concentration for the duration of the game.

b) Movement and positioning

- keep up with the play
- only umpire your allocated area (Each sport has a conventional place where the officials would take charge. Umpires in a netball game, for instance, would work as a team and make sure they only make decisions in their half of the court unless consulted.)
- know the positions for special plays.

Netball

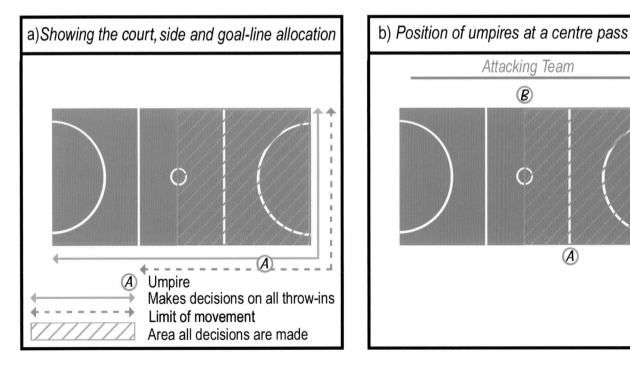

a) *Showing the court, side and goal-line allocation*

(A) Umpire
Makes decisions on all throw-ins
Limit of movement
Area all decisions are made

b) *Position of umpires at a centre pass*

Attacking Team

c) *Umpire's movement as the ball enters the circle*

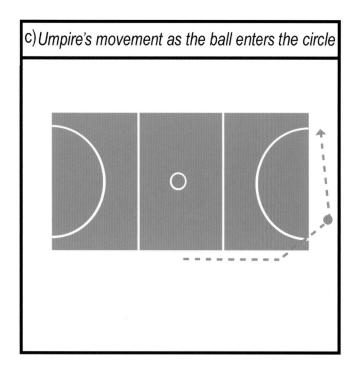

d) *Position of umpire when ball is in opposite third of court*

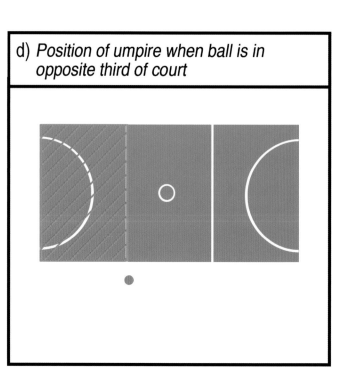

Football

c) *Position of referee at a goal kick*

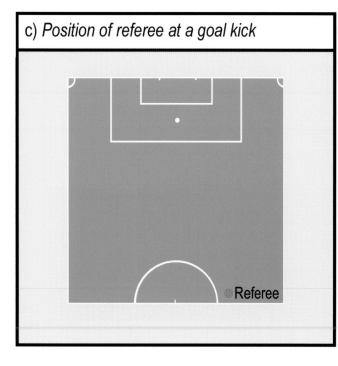

f) *Position of referee and assistant at a corner*

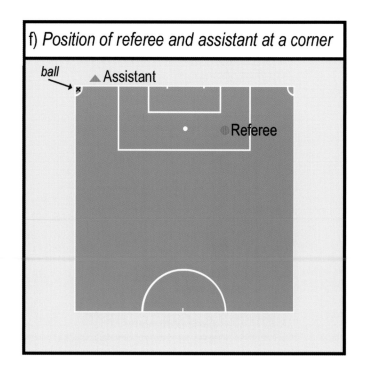

c) Observation

- have an understanding of what the game should be like and what to look out for
- watch the performance continually (In ball games, though your focus should be on the ball, your peripheral vision should be used to spot other incidents.)
- adopt the best position to see the action of the game
- use the other officials if you are unsighted.

d) Communication

- make the decisions clear and make them at the appropriate speed
- state any infringements impartially
- make clear and appropriate hand signals
- be able to defuse a confrontational or over-competitive situation

Personal skills

Umpires should be confident in their own ability resulting from study, practice and experience. When making decisions they should be clear-minded, efficient and positive so that the players know exactly what decisions are being made and the reason why. As there is only a split second to react to a situation and make a decision, umpires should be quick-minded. Even then it is still difficult, if not impossible, to be right 100 per cent of the time. Nevertheless, it is fundamentally important that their decisions are impartial and fair. The umpire's job is to make appropriate decisions quickly; if there is any doubt, then advice from the other officials can be sought. What they must not let happen, however, is for the players to influence their decisions.

In some sports, umpires need to be physically fit to keep up with the pace of the game for the duration of the match. Unlike players, umpires cannot be substituted when tired.

4 ▶ DUTIES OF A REFEREE/UMPIRE

The duties of a referee/umpire are the jobs they are expected to perform. An umpire should check that they have the correct equipment before each match so that their job can be completed effectively and efficiently. Such equipment may include:

- watch to time the play (a back-up watch is recommended)
- pencil to record the score or official decisions (spare pencils are recommended)
- score pad set out for the particular game
- disciplinary cards to be shown for foul play.

DUTIES OF A REFEREE/UMPIRE

In preparation for the game

- Have a full knowledge of the rules of the game.
- Gain experience for the standard of the match.
- Make sure personal presentation is of a high standard.
- Have all necessary equipment.
- Achieve a level of fitness to meet the demands of the game.

During the game

- Concentrate throughout the play.
- Watch play all of the time.
- Keep up with play.
- Keep play within the laws of the game.
- Work as a team with the other officials.
- Make decisions efficiently.
- Communicate clearly with players and officials.
- Keep an accurate record of the score/fouls.

Before the game

- Check the condition of the playing surface for safety.
- Check equipment:
  - match ball
  - goals.
- Check players:
  - dress
  - jewellery
  - equipment.

After the game

- Record the score.
- Make sure both teams know the final score.
- Write a match report (if necessary).
- Send scores (and report) to relevant body.

5 ▶ AN UMPIRE'S ACTIONS AT AN INFRINGEMENT

During the course of a game, infringements of the rules will occur. The players are relying on the referee to stop play and take the necessary action. The players need to see a decision and the resulting action made:

- promptly (at the time of the incident)
- clearly (so there is no doubt what the stoppage is for)
- appropriately (the decision fits the infringement)
- impartially (the same treatment is given to both sides)
- consistently (decisions are made each time they are necessary).

When an infringement occurs, the following order of actions from the official is necessary:

- see the offence
- blow the whistle
- state the offence and give the correct signal
- announce the decision and give the correct signal
- take any action
- let play commence once a decision has been made.

6 ▶ HOW TO IMPROVE YOUR KNOWLEDGE

You will have gained much knowledge already through your experience of taking part in activities and sports in PE lessons. This foundation of knowledge can be built on by tapping several sources. These will consolidate and build on what you know, increasing your understanding, technical language and knowledge of procedures necessary for the running of your chosen activity. The following list includes ways to increase your knowledge and understanding:

- watch matches on TV and video and listen to the commentary from the experts
- play the game to as high a standard as you can
- read rule books
- read coaching manuals
- discuss rules with your teacher or coach
- practise refereeing or umpiring
- shadow a referee – with their permission stand behind a referee and try to pick out the fouls as they are committed and before the whistle has been blown. You should also decide what decision you would make and see how many times you are correct
- use the Internet to find information on rules.

7 HOW TO BUILD UP UMPIRING EXPERIENCE

Despite their apparent confidence all referees have started at the same basic level. Playing any sport according to its rules over a period of time will have given you enough experience to umpire at a basic level. Be confident and have a go – the more you umpire the better you will get.

There are several ways to gain experience. You can umpire:

- a short game made up of your friends, looking for only a selection of the main infringements
- a short game looking for most of the infringements
- a full game with much younger players
- a full game with players of your own age.

8 JUDGING A COMPETITION

Many sporting activities require the judging of a performance. These tend to be individual activities where performance against a standard or compliance with definite rules is necessary for success. Such sports include: gymnastics, diving, trampolining and athletics. Generally a team or panel of judges work together to determine the success of the performance.

Gymnastics

In a floorwork routine in gymnastics, judges look for certain criteria. Four judges mark the routine out of ten. They deduct marks for errors; for example, if the required number of movements or correct level of difficulty is not included. There is also a master judge who is in charge overall and marks the performance as well. Their score is used if there is a major difference between the scores.

If the marks are in a similar range the master judge will then:

1 Collect the scores.

Judge 1: 9.50

Judge 2: 9.30

Judge 3: 9.60

Judge 4: 9.40

2 Rank the four marks.

Judge 3: 9.60

Judge 1: 9.50

Judge 4: 9.40

Judge 2: 9.30

3 Select the middle two scores and add them together.

Judge 1: 9.50

Judge 4: 9.40

Total: 18.90

4 Work out the final score (by adding the middle two scores together and then dividing by two).

Final score: 9.45

If the marks vary greatly or the middle two scores are very different the master judge will:

1 Add the master judge's score to the final score.

2 Find the average score by dividing by two. This figure is used as the base mark for the performance.

3 The judges meet and discuss their scores. The master judge will check the reasons for the difference in scores.

4 A judge may change his or her score as a result of the meeting and the base mark.

5 The calculations are made again with the new score.

Athletics

Many judges are needed to adjudicate an athletics meeting. Each track and field event needs a team of judges to make sure the rules are adhered to and the competition is fair.

For jumping-for-distance events there will be judges for the following:

- deciding whether the take-off is fair
- marking the point in the landing area where the measurement is to be made.

In major events, an operator of a wind gauge will inform the judge in charge of the event of any changes in the weather, as some records may not be valid if there is too much wind assistance.

For jumping-for-height events there will be two judges for the following:

- recording the jumps and checking the bar has been cleared after each attempt
- measuring the height of the bar after each attempt.

The high jump judge's duties:

- decides the starting height
- raises the bar 2cm each round

- replaces the bar in the same way each time
- makes sure the same side of the bar faces outwards
- informs the competitors of the change in height
- decides on failed jumps; for instance, if the competitor goes past the plane of the nearer edges of the bar without first clearing the bar
- consults with the winning competitor how far the bar is raised
- records the height to the nearest centimetre below the height measured if the distance is not a whole centimetre
- decides on the placing if there is a tie.

The sprint relay judge's duties:

In the sprint relay race the change-over judge's job is brief but quick and accurate decisions must be made to ensure the safety and fairness of the competition. There are several duties of a change-over judge:

- allows competitors one check mark in their lane
- makes sure the baton is carried by the competitor in one hand throughout the race (If the baton is dropped, then it can be picked up by the person who drops it. The runner is allowed to leave the lane to retrieve it as long as they do not impede any other runner and the distance run is no shorter.)
- checks that the baton is passed within the take-over zone (The passing starts as soon as it touches the receiver's hand and finishes when it is in the hand of the receiver. Any change-overs outside the markers result in disqualification.)
- makes sure the incoming runners remain in their lanes until the coast is clear to avoid impeding other runners (disqualification is given for any hindrance)
- makes sure the incoming runner does not assist the outgoing runner by pushing them (otherwise the team will be disqualified).

CONCLUSION

When deciding which sport to analyse and officiate, choose the one you are good at and feel you know the rules of best. Take into account your own experience in the activity and make the effort to gain further knowledge and practise as you go along.

The duties of the officials, when done well, help the smooth running of the activity. The players are relying on the referee or umpire to apply the rules consistently, efficiently and positively. This will allow the players to concentrate on their game, knowing that the game will be kept safe, fair and entertaining.

2 APPRECIATING THE ROLE OF RULES

This section contains:

1. ▷ What rules do
2. ▷ Rules keeping the game safe
3. ▷ Rules making the game entertaining
4. ▷ Rules making the game fair
5. ▷ A player's chances
6. ▷ Regulations

1 ▷ WHAT RULES DO

- Keep the game safe.
- Make the game fair.
- Give the game its individual characteristics.
- Make the game entertaining.

In some sports the rules are called laws, but they do the same job. Even games that have similar skills are made different due to the particular rules that govern them. Racket sports like tennis, badminton and squash all have the fundamental aim of hitting the missile into an area where the opponent is not, but the rules on the racket, missile, court and the specific skills make the games completely different.

The rules of a game exist to make it fair and safe for both teams or players. There is usually a series of procedures in place to penalise foul play, persistent foul play and unacceptable conduct. A graduated procedure of punishment exists to stop a team gaining an unfair advantage by continually infringing the rules. Penalising foul play helps to maintain the well-being of the players.

Many rules in sport have developed over the years to allow the competition to be exciting and entertaining. Recent changes in the format of some games have been made with the onset of TV coverage and the demand for a quicker result.

2 ▷ RULES KEEPING THE GAME SAFE

Hockey

The stick is an extension of the player's arms. The shape, material and way in which the stick is used make it a potentially dangerous piece of equipment. There are rules governing the use of the stick to help keep the game **safe**.

Approximate line for dangerous play

The rules state that 'a player may not raise his or her stick dangerously, to intimidate or hamper another player whether they are approaching, attempting to play, playing or stopping the ball'.

There are also rules governing the ball. Its size, shape, composition and the strength with which it can be hit make it a dangerous piece of equipment. It is an infringement to hit the ball at an opponent, to raise the ball dangerously or play the ball intentionally at an opposition foot, leg or ankle.

In both cases the innocent team gets the advantage of possession of the ball and setting up a play from a dead-ball situation.

3 ▸ RULES MAKING THE GAME ENTERTAINING

Badminton

One aspect that contributes to the entertainment value of a game of badminton is the rallying, where the players attempt to out-manoeuvre their opponents. The players are relatively close during the game, especially at the service. If the service had an overarm action then it would be almost impossible to return. This would reduce the entertainment, as there would be no competitive rallies. The rules governing the service action, to ensure an underarm serve, are therefore as follows:

- the shuttle must be struck below the level of the waist
- the shaft of the racket should be pointing in a downward direction on contact with the shuttle
- the flight of the shuttle should be in an upward direction.

Despite the rules tightly controlling the action, there is scope for variation as the player can serve high, low or use a flick serve to try to outwit their opponent.

Basketball

In basketball, there are rules that make the game more attacking and therefore more of a spectacle. When a team gains possession of a ball in their half they have eight seconds to pass the ball into their attacking half. At the same time, they have 24 seconds to attempt a shot. If they go over either of the time limits then possession is given to the opposition.

4 RULES MAKING THE GAME FAIR

Football

The game of football is very physical and highly competitive. It is inevitable that fouls will occur during the game. To prevent teams fouling to gain an unfair advantage, the laws of the game dealing with foul play are highly structured. There are different categories of infringement – some warranting a yellow or red card being shown. Each infringement gives the fouled team a type of free kick in order to try to redress the balance:

- indirect free kicks – for obstruction
- direct free kicks – for fouls against other players, time wasting or misconduct
- penalty kicks – for foul play happening in the penalty area.

5 A PLAYER'S CHANCES

During a game of football, a player will have many chances to play in a fair and safe way before they are disqualified from the game.

- A player who fouls another player has a free or indirect free kick awarded against them.
- If fouling persists or a cautionable offence is committed for the first time, then a yellow card is awarded.
- Two yellow card offences or the committing of a sending-off offence results in a red card being shown and the player must leave the field of play.

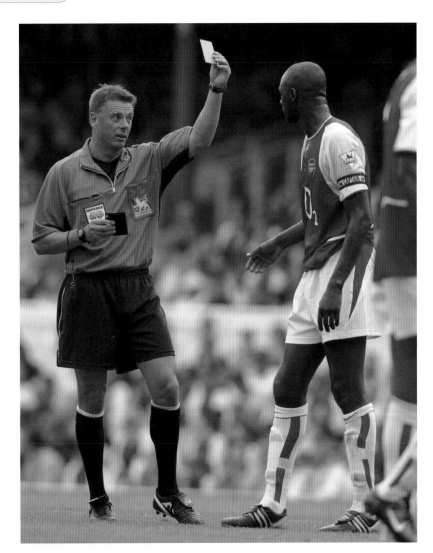

▶ *Patrick Vieira is shown the yellow card by referee Mark Halsey.*

6 ▷ REGULATIONS

Regulations are similar to rules, but are usually about specific requirements of the game. Examples of regulations include: the correct equipment, the size of the playing area and the players' dress code. Regulations set guidelines that those involved in the sport must adhere to, usually before the action of the game commences.

▲ *Regulations are established in rugby to ensure that players play in an atmosphere of safety.*

CONCLUSION

There will be many rules in your chosen game. The mix of rules governing each sport gives each activity its individuality. Each rule has been designed to make the game safe, fair and entertaining. It is important to be familiar with the rules and understand what effect they have on the game.

3 USING THE CORRECT TERMINOLOGY

This section contains:

1. ▷ Communication
2. ▷ Specialised terminology
3. ▷ Technical terms

Terminology is the specialised vocabulary used for an activity. As the game is in progress, the players need to react to the opposition, play as a team and change tactics if necessary. For this to happen successfully, they need to be able to communicate with each other quickly and efficiently and know exactly what is meant by signals and keywords. For each sport, a specialised vocabulary has developed. Everyone involved in a particular activity uses the same words, which means that communication is clear and easy between players, coaches and officials.

1 ▶ COMMUNICATION

It is important that all those involved in the activity understand each other. Once the language of the sport is learnt, then a greater level of communication is available. In cricket, for example, there are 30 different fielding positions. The captain will redirect his fielders to different positions during the game. To field in some positions needs great skill, so players often specialise in a particular position. Although some of these field placements are fairly close to each other, all are there to support a particular bowler and form the attack. The attack is set for the type of bowling – a fast bowler will have fielders in 'fine' positions and the slower bowler will have straighter and squarer fielders. Understanding the language of the sport breaks down the barriers and the terms used will help to explain the skills, tactics and rules clearly.

▲ *A basketball coach will clearly give instructions to the team using the language of the activity.*

Each group of people involved in an activity needs to understand the terminology for different reasons:

For the teacher – to introduce and develop the skills and tactics to the players.

For the players – to work together and understand the tactics and plays during the game.

For the coach – to explain the tactics and call out the plays during the activity.

For the referee – to communicate with the players and call the infringements with the correct terminology.

For the analyser – to feed back to the player in the familiar language of the sport/activity.

For the spectator – to appreciate the game in the fullest way.

2 SPECIALISED TERMINOLOGY

For each activity, there is a specialised terminology. This helps the communication between teachers, players, coaches and officials. It is important to have a command of the language of the game you have chosen, so that you have an understanding of the rules, infringements, tactics, skills and strategies.

Verbal

Each game has a bank of words that describe a specific action, type of play or piece of equipment. Although different sports have similar skills, the terms used for each sport will be unique to that game. Basketball and netball have restrictions on the amount of steps a player can take. In netball, the infringement is called **footwork**, in basketball it is called **travelling**.

Non-verbal

For most sports, there is a series of hand signals accompanying the official's decisions. These form a visual terminology designed to make any decision made clear to the players and spectators. Each sport has its own bank of hand signals used when rules are infringed. After a foul has been committed, the referee/umpire will give a hand signal to make sure all players, even those far from the action, know what is happening. All of the hand signals are in the official rule book of the sport.

As well as the official signals given by officials like referees and linesmen, coaches and players may have their own set of signals. These signals are private and great effort can sometimes be taken to keep their meaning secret.

▶ *Coaches can relay information on tactics to their team using a series of signals.*

3 TECHNICAL TERMS

Technical terms can describe a type of shot, part of a playing area, piece of equipment or body action necessary for the action to take place. Each activity has its own set of technical terms. There may be some similarity in the equipment used in different sports; however they will be known differently. For example, both basketball and netball have boundary lines at the ends of the court, but one is called the base line (basketball) and the other the goal line. Showing a command of the correct technical terms and the ability to use them appropriately will show knowledge and understanding of your chosen activity.

Badminton

Badminton has its own set of technical terminology covering types of shot, actions used and types of play. The coach or teacher will refer to these during a training session and will therefore build up the technical language of the performer.

The types of play

Singles

As the singles court is long and thin, players concentrate on alternating between drop shots and overhead clears to make their opponents move the greatest distances. By putting their opponents under pressure in this way, opportunities to play a winning smash usually arise.

Doubles

In doubles, players attempt to dominate the rally by adopting the front/back attacking formation. By playing the shuttle to the sides of the court, they force their opponents into the side, which leaves them more vulnerable as there are more spaces to hit the shuttle into.

The shots

The following list contains a series of overhead shots a player would use during a game:

High clear – shuttle hit with a high trajectory to reach the back tramlines, usually played in defence.

Standard clear – shuttle hit with a slightly lower trajectory than the high clear, but still reaches the back tramlines, usually played as part of the rally when the players are not under pressure.

Attacking clear – shuttle hit with a lower trajectory to reach the back tramlines, usually played as an attacking shot.

Fast drop shot – shuttle hit with a low trajectory to land quickly front to mid-court to win a rally or make the opposition hit the shuttle in an upward direction so that their lifted shot may be smashed and the rally won.

Slow drop shot – shuttle hit with a higher trajectory to land just over and close to the net to win a rally or make the opposition hit the shuttle in an upward direction so that their return can be smashed.

Steep smash – shuttle hit with a steep downward angle to land quickly front to mid-court to win a rally or make the opposition play a defensive shot.

Long smash – shuttle hit with a less steep angle in a downward direction to land near the back tramlines to win a rally or make the opposition play a defensive shot.

The action

Apart from the movement of the body when playing shots, good footwork is necessary to enable efficient movement around the court. The following are examples of recognised types of footwork for badminton:

Lunge – after running forwards to the shuttle, the last step is longer and stabilising so that the shot can be played with control and the player can move back easily to reposition.

Chassé – quick foot movements made to travel around the court without crossing over the feet.

Split jump – a stabilising jump, stopping the previous movement so that a change of direction can be made efficiently.

The court

The badminton court has special names for the areas of play and line markings of the court (see opposite page).

CONCLUSION

Your chosen activity will have its own, individual language describing the skills, tactics, court and rules involved. It is important to be familiar with and be able to use the right language when communicating with others about your activity. Having a command of the language of the activity will lead to better, in-depth communication for those involved. When describing the skills, use the correct technical terms for the action, court, tactics and equipment.

Areas of Play on a Badminton Court

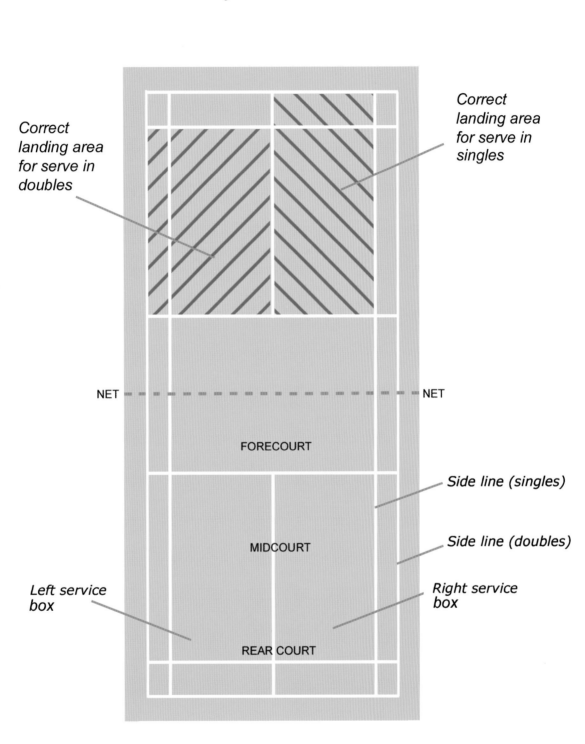

Correct landing area for serve in doubles

Correct landing area for serve in singles

NET — — — — — NET

FORECOURT

Side line (singles)

MIDCOURT

Side line (doubles)

Left service box

Right service box

REAR COURT

4 OBSERVATION AND ANALYSIS

1 CHOOSING THE RIGHT ACTIVITY TO ANALYSE

Many people can watch an activity but only the trained eye can understand the skills and actions of the performance. The observation and analysis part of the course requires you to train these observation skills and make judgements on quality, success, and ways of improving a performance.

You can choose any activity to analyse. You are likely to find that the activity that you are most familiar with, in terms of experience and knowledge of the rules, is likely to be the easiest one to tackle. The more you know about your activity, the better the foundation from which to observe and analyse.

Your personal experiences of playing, being coached and observing top quality performances should give you a clear understanding of what the activity should look like when performed correctly.

2 GAINING OBSERVATIONAL EXPERIENCE AND UNDERSTANDING

There are different ways you can build up your observational skills and understanding of an activity. Using as many methods as you can will give you the broadest information base from which to work.

- Know as much about the activity as possible. This will allow you to anticipate the action, prepare a mental picture of the best performance and compare it with what you see. The expectation of the action aids an understanding of how effective the performance observed has been.

- Watch top class play of the activity, live or recorded.

- Discuss a performance with others to develop knowledge, language and understanding of what you see.
- Listen to the coaching points given by your teacher in class or coaches at your club and compare them with how a person performs the activity. This will develop your experience of linking the description of the correct action with a beginner's attempt.
- Read appropriate coaching manuals and books. This will give you knowledge of what the perfect model should look like. When comparing this knowledge with the novice performer, the differences will become apparent and will therefore develop your observational skills.
- Understand the components of skill required in order to perform well.
- Video class performance and study what you see. You can then build up your observation and appreciation of the whole action after several replays.
- Study photographs of sports performers who are expert in their sport.
- Study the progression of time-lapsed photography.
- Watch specialised coaching productions on video or CD-ROM.

3 PLAN YOUR OBSERVATION

Choose the best place from which to view. Different positions will give a different view of the action; more than one viewpoint may be necessary for a full picture of an activity. In many cases, a raised position allows you to see more.

Have the correct equipment at hand – record sheets, pencils (pencils are better for outside as they keep working in the rain!) and something to lean on are all basic and obvious requirements to do the job.

Work out which key points you need to watch; this will help you focus your observation. You may prefer to photograph or video the performance. In which case, greater planning is necessary in order to book the equipment before the date.

4 EXPECTATIONS OF THE OBSERVER

Many factors can influence a performance. These are sometimes in the control of the performer and sometimes not. When observing an activity a distinction should be made between the two, and comments and feedback given should be adapted accordingly. For instance, a player may well have shown success or great skill in an activity in the past, but changes in the weather could cause the skill to break down, for example the ball toss for the serve in tennis might be a problem on a very windy day but at no other time.

ALWAYS HAVE IN MIND THE PERFECT MODEL	FACTORS AFFECTING THE PERFORMER	REACTION AND COMMENTS MADE APPROPRIATELY

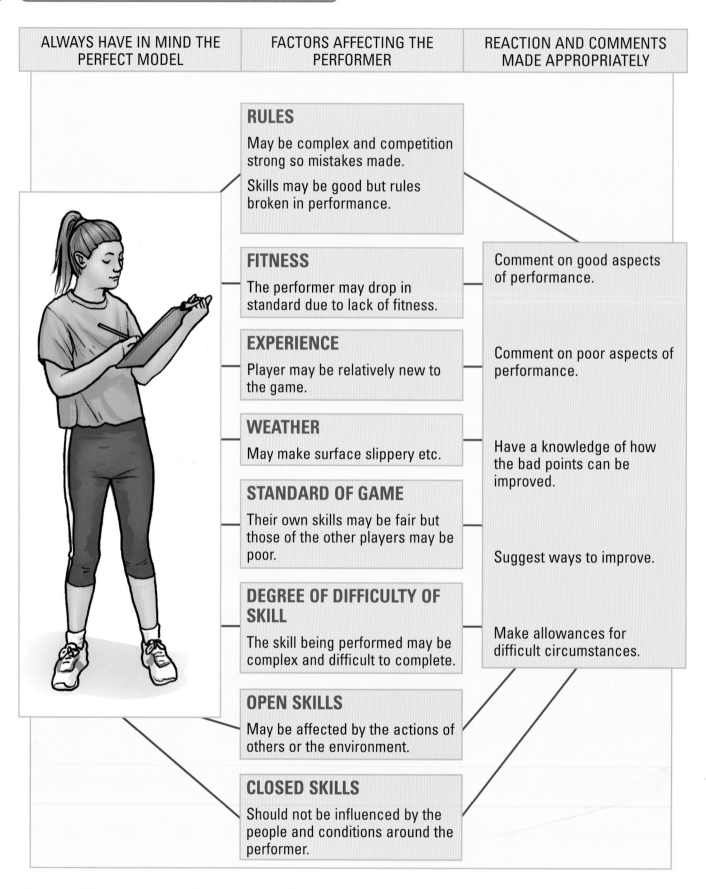

RULES

May be complex and competition strong so mistakes made.

Skills may be good but rules broken in performance.

FITNESS

The performer may drop in standard due to lack of fitness.

EXPERIENCE

Player may be relatively new to the game.

WEATHER

May make surface slippery etc.

STANDARD OF GAME

Their own skills may be fair but those of the other players may be poor.

DEGREE OF DIFFICULTY OF SKILL

The skill being performed may be complex and difficult to complete.

OPEN SKILLS

May be affected by the actions of others or the environment.

CLOSED SKILLS

Should not be influenced by the people and conditions around the performer.

Comment on good aspects of performance.

Comment on poor aspects of performance.

Have a knowledge of how the bad points can be improved.

Suggest ways to improve.

Make allowances for difficult circumstances.

▲ *Factors influencing the expectations and reactions of the observer.*

5 KNOWLEDGE OF SKILL-RELATED FITNESS

What you have learnt about skill-related fitness and its application to different sports will help with your observations. You will know which components to look out for in your chosen activity. This knowledge will enable you to break down the action into smaller parts, helping you to analyse.

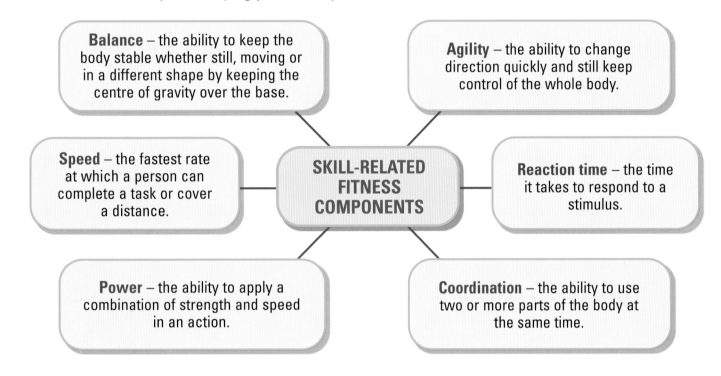

Balance – the ability to keep the body stable whether still, moving or in a different shape by keeping the centre of gravity over the base.

Agility – the ability to change direction quickly and still keep control of the whole body.

Speed – the fastest rate at which a person can complete a task or cover a distance.

SKILL-RELATED FITNESS COMPONENTS

Reaction time – the time it takes to respond to a stimulus.

Power – the ability to apply a combination of strength and speed in an action.

Coordination – the ability to use two or more parts of the body at the same time.

▲ *Each sport has its own combination of skill components necessary for success.*

6 THE PERFECT MODEL

In order to realise whether the action is good, an appreciation of how the action should look in its perfect state should be understood. Any analysis should be marked against this 'perfect model'. There are several ways you can observe the perfect model:

- watching top/world class sports coverage
- studying training videos/CD-ROMs
- reading coaching manuals
- studying action photos from media publications of world class players
- looking at specialist sites on the Internet.

Watching video recordings of matches and performances of top performers can help develop an understanding of the perfect model. By replaying, slowing and pausing the action, you can fully appreciate the performance in question.

When looking at a performance, the shape of the body in action will indicate how close it is to the 'perfect model'. Some areas to look for are the head position, where the centre of gravity is, a balanced body position and how the weight is distributed.

Take every opportunity to compare, at length, evidence of the performance to the perfect model.

Colin Jackson

- Head placed low in a forward position
- Lead leg outstretched forward
- Arm still in running action
- Body leaning forwards and low
- Shoulders square
- Trail leg close to hurdle
- Whole body close to hurdle going forwards

Schoolboy

- Head high
- Lead leg bent
- Arm too far to the side
- Body upright
- Shoulders turned
- Trail leg – knee position at an angle
- Whole body too high and going upwards

7 ANALYSING PERFORMANCE

To successfully analyse performance you need to be able to recognise the strengths and weaknesses of a performance, and understand and demonstrate ways to improve them. Analysis is part of the whole process a coach would use in order to improve a person's performance.

The Coaching Model has all the components for what you need to study for this section. The following coaching model is useful when breaking down the parts that are important for analysis.

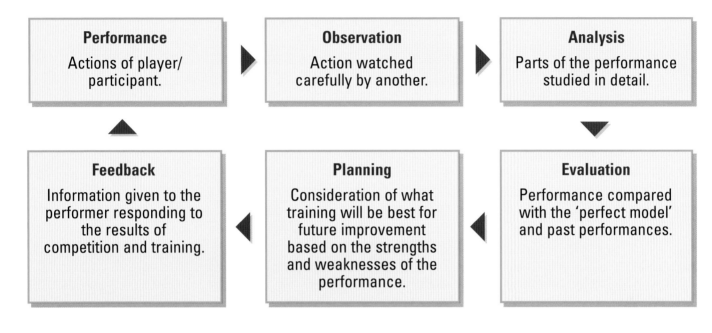

Performance	**Observation**	**Analysis**
Actions of player/ participant.	Action watched carefully by another.	Parts of the performance studied in detail.

Feedback	**Planning**	**Evaluation**
Information given to the performer responding to the results of competition and training.	Consideration of what training will be best for future improvement based on the strengths and weaknesses of the performance.	Performance compared with the 'perfect model' and past performances.

▲ *An interpretation of the Coaching Model.*

8 ▶ WAYS TO ANALYSE

Comments made on a performance can be based on a person's opinion or factual evidence: each can comment about the same action but in a different way.

Subjective

Subjective analysis is related to how the observer thinks the player is performing in comparison with the other players. This type of analysis is based on opinion. As two people may have a different opinion about a performance, a bank of reasons why you have that opinion is necessary. Examples of subjective statements are:

'That's the best goal I've seen him score.'

'She looks to be serving better.'

'He is moving quicker to the ball.'

'I thought that shot had more pace.'

'There seem to be fewer double faults than in previous sets.'

'She is crossing the ball better.'

'He has more energy than the others.'

Objective

Objective analysis is based on fact, not personal opinions. The aim of this type of analysis is to have results and statistics to back up the observations. This is very helpful to the coach and performer, as it identifies explicitly the strengths and weaknesses of the performer. Objective analysis provides:

- a statistical record of aspects of the performance
- records of heights jumped, distances thrown, speeds run or number of successful attempts at a particular skill
- comparisons made between the performer and the decided criteria (perfect model).

9 ▶ WHAT CAN BE ANALYSED?

There is a variety of areas that can be analysed when looking at performance. Some are more complex than others. The most straightforward are individual, closed and basic skills; the most complicated are open, complex and advanced skills.

There are different skills required by different players on the pitch so the observer must be mindful of this in the analysis. An attacker may not need information on the number of tackles they make, but for a defender, this would be an important part of the analysis. A strong team may be often on the attack, so the defence is only rarely involved. As a result, a defender may only make a few passes in the game, so for them, the percentage rather than the actual number of successful passes made may reveal more about their personal play.

▶ *The skills required for good play are different for a defender and attacker.*

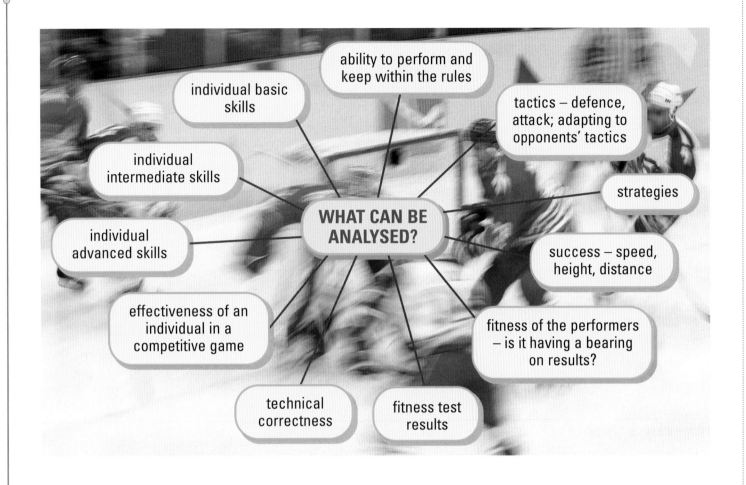

individual basic skills

ability to perform and keep within the rules

tactics – defence, attack; adapting to opponents' tactics

individual intermediate skills

strategies

WHAT CAN BE ANALYSED?

individual advanced skills

success – speed, height, distance

effectiveness of an individual in a competitive game

fitness of the performers – is it having a bearing on results?

technical correctness

fitness test results

CONCLUSION

When preparing to analyse be mindful of the following:

- have an idea of the types of comments you are going to make
  - subjective
  - objective
- begin by assessing straightforward 'closed' skills
- attempt 'open skill' assessment once you are more experienced
- analyse the player on the skills most relevant for their position
- compare what you see with what is considered to be an ideal or expert performance of the same skill or activity (the perfect model)
- remember, the whole team may be losing, but the player you are assessing could be having a good game
- record your findings and keep them safe for future reference.

5 RECOGNISING STRENGTHS AND WEAKNESSES

This section contains:

1. ▸ The perfect model
2. ▸ Evaluate a performance by comparing it with the perfect model
3. ▸ Knowledge of the activity
4. ▸ Athletics example
5. ▸ Football example
6. ▸ Netball example

1 THE PERFECT MODEL

The perfect model is how top class performers perform the activity at their best. The image of such skills and abilities should be clear in your mind when completing your analysis of performance.

Your knowledge of the activity will also provide you with an image of what the action should look like. A good knowledge and practical experience of the activity will lead to a more comprehensive understanding of how the activity should be performed.

You should understand the various types of skill and conditioning the activity relies on for success. Is it necessary for a player to change direction quickly, work at a moderate-to-hard rate for long periods or is their hand-eye coordination essential?

Usually an activity will require a mixture of skills, types of fitness and body conditioning.

2 EVALUATE A PERFORMANCE BY COMPARING IT WITH THE PERFECT MODEL

This is the process after analysis when the coach or observer works out the success or failure of an activity. Evaluation tells us where strengths and weaknesses are and how training should be adapted to the findings in order to make progress.

Knowledge of the perfect model may come from a photograph, video or coaching manual. Understanding the perfect model will make it easier to evaluate what is seen and suggest improvements to be made.

The evaluation process may look like this:

1 Perfect model – know what you are looking for.

2 Make observations of the performance.

3 Compare the performance with the perfect model.

4 Decide on and state the main positive point to express.

5 Decide on and state the main fault and express it.

6 Communicate how the performance can be improved at the next attempt (short term).

7 Communicate how training will need to be adapted and a new plan made (mid term).

8 See changes in the performance in a targeted event or competition (long term).

head position (eyes watching ball)

alignment of the body

centre of gravity (low and over base)

correct body shape

grip on the stick

feet position

balanced and stable base

▲ *Factors building up to the perfect model.*

3 ▸ KNOWLEDGE OF THE ACTIVITY

Each activity has its own special combination of skills, skill-related components and body conditioning. Identifying these areas will give an idea of the parts of the body and the body systems required to train and develop for success. It is essential to know what is needed in the sport in order to include the correct methods, exercises and practices in training. This knowledge can then be adapted to an individual performer to form a workable and relevant personal exercise programme (**PEP**) for them.

The analysis section will give you an example of how to apply the following to a variety of activities:

- Knowledge
- Training principles
- Training methods
- Training practices

Suggestions of how to monitor and evaluate progress will also be given. In order to use the information for your own chosen activity and give the best response for your final exam mark, you will be required to adapt the text by applying your own understanding, knowledge and personal experience to the chosen area.

You may feel the need to develop your knowledge and understanding of your chosen activity. Do this by:

- reading coaching manuals to increase your knowledge
- using Internet sites for up-to-date information on training
- watching coaching videos or CD-ROMs
- discussing coaching points with your teacher or coach
- developing your own skills to the highest standard
- watching top class performers.

4 ▶ ATHLETICS EXAMPLE – SHOT PUT

When first starting to perform the shot put a person will rely on their natural ability to do the best they can. For a person to improve and progress further, particular components of skill-related fitness, health-related fitness and personal qualities need to be developed. By concentrating on these areas in training, the performer has the best chance to reach his or her potential in the event. The following guidelines are some of the main areas particular to shot put that a person needs to work on.

▲ *A young athlete learns how to throw the shot put.*

Know what makes up your chosen sport

What makes a successful shot putter?

Skill-related fitness

- Strength – of the muscles to resist the force of the shot
- Speed – combining with strength to make power
- Balance – to start the action under control and giving a position to move effectively from
- Agility – to cross the circle and shift the weight in a controlled way
- Power – for a single, explosive action extending the arm (combining strength and speed)

Health-related fitness

- Flexibility – needed at the hips to turn the body with forward momentum so the arm is moving forwards and upwards at release
- Body composition – big build with large muscle and heavy weight
- Muscular strength – able to perform a single maximum contraction to overcome resistance

Personal qualities

- Ambition
- Discipline
- Determination
- Self belief
- Confidence
- Single-mindedness
- Good under pressure

Be able to identify the perfect model

The perfect model

This event is unique to other athletic activities. As a result it has certain skills, progressions and training methods linked with it. The knowledge of the event and the performer influences the coach to set out an individual programme, hopefully maximising success.

▲ *A time-lapsed illustration of the shot put.*

Know how the action is made up of small parts

Breaking down the action

When analysing the action, be mindful of the different phases making up the whole action. The performer should remember that the throw is the combination of force starting from the slower, stronger muscles of the legs and pelvis, to the faster but weaker muscles of the shoulders and arms. The following outline breaks down the action for the shift style of putting for a right-handed thrower:

Grip – shot placed at base of three, outspread fingers with the thumb and little finger supporting.

Stance – shot placed in contact with the neck and elbow raised high.

Crouch – facing the back of the circle, weight on right leg, body low and closed, left knee brought in close to the right.

Shift – lean body towards the toe board, drive back on right leg whilst extending left leg vigorously, keeping body low and rotating the hips outwards so at right angles with closed shoulders.

Put position – weight transfers from back to front leg, pushing hips to the front, right leg extends (causing the lift).

Lift – left arm swings down and back, right shoulder driven outwards.

Strike – when shoulders square, with elbow high, arm punches the shot out at the last moment as a result of the leg and hip action (left shoulder kept high too).

Release – approximately 40 degrees (elite athletes release at 30–40 degrees) with elbow high and on line with the shot, arm punches forward and wrist flips, causing the thumb to point downwards.

Recovery – once shot is released, right leg moves to the front to stop forward motion.

Know the building blocks for the action

Building up the action

The parts of the whole action can be split up and trained individually. Concentrating on part of the action and building the movements up can be useful when working with performers of any level of ability. With the novice, the following order may be used:

– the singular parts can be practised on their own

– link the skills together

– add pace to the skills.

For the better performer, once the weakness in the action has been identified, that particular part can be focused on and singled out for concentrated attention in a similar way as for the novice.

When starting out in the shot put event, there is a series of logical progressions to learn and practise that follow on from one another and build up to the action.

Knowledge of these may help once the action has been analysed and the weaknesses identified. The particular progression can be selected and worked on in a training session.

The following are shot put teaching progressions for a right-hander:

1 Grip.

2 Position of shot under the chin in contact with the neck.

3 Train the correct wrist action by putting the shot down to the ground.

4 Delivery – facing forward, both feet pointing towards the throw area, weight on bent right leg, transfer weight to toes of left leg and deliver the shot.

5 Cross-step with put action.

6 Step forward once and put action.

7 One step back and put action.

8 Series of glides in a straight line.

9 Glide in the circle to markings pre-drawn.

▲ *British shot put record holder, Judy Oakes, focuses on leg technique with her coach Mike Winch.*

10 Use the glide and the put action together.

11 Hop on the right leg, tucking it under the body at a right angle.

12 Pivot on a 15cm platform.

13 As above adding the put action.

14 Glide from the elevated platform and throw.

15 Glide and throw under a high jump bar for a low power position.

> **Adapt a warm-up to your chosen sport**

Suitable warm-up

As with all sports it is important to warm up prior to training or the event. The whole body should be warmed up aerobically first, followed by static stretching exercises, using the muscles involved in the action of the activity, including: quadriceps, hamstrings, gluteals, abdominals, latissimus dorsi, pectorals, deltoids, biceps and triceps. Dynamic stretching exercises are then completed in order to get the joints moving and improve flexibility, and after these, more skills-based work links the general and specific action. Lastly, when the body is ready, more intense work can be attempted, for example sprints. Remember injury may occur if strenuous actions are attempted too early.

Psychologically, the warm-up will focus the mind of the performer and will help him or her to prepare mentally for the competition.

▶ *Jogging and sidestepping can be used in the aerobic phase of the warm-up.*

STATIC STRETCHES

Quadriceps Stretch

Lying Hip Abductor

Hip Bends

Lying on floor, leg reaches
over to floor on opposite side

Arm out for balance
(or place hand on wall),
bend one leg behind
and pull ankle towards
buttocks

Leg crosses over and body twists round

▲ *Flexibility exercises help to loosen up the muscles around the joints.*

In brief, this is the order a warm-up should take:

Aerobic phase (5–10 minutes) – jogging or sidestepping to increase body temperature.

Flexibility phase (5–10 minutes) – **static stretches** to reduce muscle stiffness.

Stretch phase (5–10 minutes) – **dynamic (moving) stretches** to reduce muscle stiffness.

Skill phase (10–15 minutes) – specific drills for the sport – upper body/lower body/technique drills, for example:

a) holding the shot in both hands in front of the body, lifting the shot up and out

b) pushing the shot out like a basketball chest pass

c) pushing the shot from the put position using only the wrist (to warm up the wrist).

Increased intensity phase (2 minutes) – working on technique with greater intensity, imitating the action used in the event now performed at speed:

a) lighter weighted shot substitutes can be used

b) practise full speed glide action without the shot.

DYNAMIC STRETCHES

Flexing/Relaxing

Alternate heels to flex and relax

Lifting/Lowering

Knee lifts and lowers

Swinging

Alternate legs swinging 10 times forwards and backwards

Rotating

Different teachers and coaches use different types of stretches. Before designing your programme check which type your teacher would prefer you to use.

AVOID ANY POSITION OF DISCOMFORT!

▲ *Flexing, relaxing, lifting, lowering and rotating parts make up this phase.*

Remember an appropriate cool down to prevent following discomfort

Cool down

5–10 minutes jogging or walking:

- helps to gradually decrease body temperature
- removes waste from the body.

5–10 minutes **static stretching**:

- decreases body temperature
- allows the muscles to relax
- helps prevent **DOMS** (delayed onset muscle soreness)
- reduces the chance of dizziness and fainting as it stops blood pooling and reduces the level of adrenalin in the blood.

▶ *Static stretches help the performer's body recover after the training session or competition.*

ANALYSIS EXAMPLE

The next section of work concentrates on how a candidate could go about analysing an athlete in action. The scenario for the activity imitates what a student may observe whilst watching the performance. There then follows three examples of responses given for each of the following boards – AQA, Edexcel and OCR.

Scenario for the shot put example

An analysis of a performance can be made from a live performance, video, coaching CD-ROM or photographs. In this case the performance is described in the following, short passage.

> The performer begins well and adopts a good grip and starting position. The crouch is held and the 'T' position is balanced and compact. The action that followed was fairly accurate in body shape and direction of movement, but it lacked sufficient speed to push the shot far. The hips turned sufficiently and at the right time. The shift backwards was slow and unsteady and the arm action lacked speed.

The following pages are responses made to the above scenario and give examples that could be used for each exam board (AQA, Edexcel and OCR). The layout and wording of the analysis sheets make every attempt to include all of the criteria stated in the examination specification. Every attempt has been made to use the terminology for that board.

AQA Analysis of Performance Form – Athletics – Shot put

Candidate	Sam Smith	Date	20/03/04	Analysis attempt	First	Own / others' performance
Activity	Athletics – shot put	Playing position	Right-handed	Experience	4 years	Playing conditions Dry, clear day

Analysis of performance

Comments

1. **Strength 1** — Good starting stance giving a balanced and stable base.

2. **Strength 2** — Good grip conforming to the rules of the sport and giving the best chance for a good action.

3. **Weakness 1** — Execution of release at a slow pace reducing the power of the action and subsequent distance.

4. **Weakness 2** — Unsteady shift backwards misaligning the body, reducing balance and making the action less efficient.

Skill-related fitness needed

Balance – gives a stable base from which to complete the action and put the shot.

Agility – able to move across circle and change direction whilst keeping balance and control.

Power (a combination of strength and speed) – pushing the shot as far as possible.

Understanding the activity

Parts of the whole action:

Grip – placement of fingers and thumb on shot (3 fingers behind the shot and little finger and thumb supporting underneath).

Stance – feet straight on to the back of the circle/hips square/shoulders closed and square/shot close into side of neck, elbow away from the torso.

Crouch – Legs bent/Free arm closed and square, close to the rear leg – 'T' position.

Shift – right leg drives backwards off heel/left leg kicks towards stop board/Free arm closed and square to the rear/eyes focused on back of circle.

Put position – head and shoulder facing back/chin, knee and toe all in line/weight shot over right foot/Free arm and shoulder closed.

Lift – head facing back/right leg lifts to drive/hips drive to the front/left leg starts bent, extends to straighten/Free arm high.

Strike – right elbow high/hips pushed to the front/right foot and left leg extended to brace the action/chest pushed up/head looks up.

Release – head looks up/chest pushed out/hips forward/left leg straightened and braced/angle of release = 41 degrees.

Nature/cause of strength/weakness

Improving performance

1. Correct stance has been understood and is repeated each time.

2. Correct grip has been understood and is repeated each time.

3. Although the action is quite accurate the performer does not understand the need for speed in the action/has not enough strength to perform the action quickly/the correct muscles have not been trained to perform the action in the correct way.

4. The performer finds it difficult to move backwards and keep balanced – muscles need practice to keep control and shape whilst in backward motion.

Targets for progress	Measuring	Monitoring
Improve explosive strength. Weight training - by lifting heavy weights quickly, concentrating on upper body and leg strength to gradually increase strength and speed.	Use 'weight training repetitions' for beginners or 'pyramid sets' for experienced performers.	After three weeks re-measure/test strength - alter the weights accordingly.
Balance body throughout the action.	Starting slowly gradually building up the pace. Count number of attempts that show good balance. Attempt each level of corrective measure 10 times.	For each attempt, record area of body that becomes misaligned and feed back to performer.

Corrective measures | **Practice set up**

Explosive Power -
a) Follow chosen weight training programme (lifting heavy weights a few times).
b) Isolate arm extension. Perform in a correct and controlled way starting slowly, gradually increasing pace.
c) Link arm action with chest extension part of the action, again gradually building up pace.

Balance -
Practise the following actions starting slowly and gradually building up the pace:
1 Repeat ten times in a row a series of three leg kicks/shifts.
2 i) Without the shot ii) With lightweight substitute (soft ball) iii) With the correctly weighted shot perform the following:
a) Adopt stance and balance on one leg
b) Swing leg
c) Swing leg and shift backwards
d) Shift backwards and plant on to other foot

Repetitive practice needs to be checked by the coach/teacher.

The performer can use a self-check system but regular monitoring is required by the coach/teacher.

Edexcel Analysis Form

Candidate Sam Smith	**Date** 20/03/04	**Analysis attempt** First	**Own/others' performance**

Activity Athletics - shot put	**Playing position** R/handed	**Experience** 4 years	**Conditions** Dry, clear day

Observation

1 Good starting stance
2 Good grip
3 Unsteady shift backwards
4 Execution of the release too slow
5 Shot drops too early

How viewed

Live game
Live practice
Video
Photo
Time-lapsed photo

Analysis – Important components of health/skill-related fitness

Balance - giving a stable base from which to complete the action and put the shot.

Agility - being able to move across the circle and change direction whilst keeping balance and control.

Power (made from a combination of strength and speed) - pushing the shot as far as possible.

Understand the action of a perfect model	**Evaluation**
The whole action has 8 parts	
Grip - 3 fingers behind and thumb and little finger supporting underneath.	Grip - correct
Stance - shoulders square, right foot straight, free leg, balancing body.	Stance - good
Crouch - legs flexed and arm closed and square to rear leg ('T' position).	Crouch - correct
Shift - right leg drives backwards off heel - towards the kick board, free arm closed and square to rear, eyes looking at the back of the circle.	Shift - from toe, too slow and free arm is out to the side
Put position - head and shoulders facing the back of the circle, chin, knee and toe in a line, weight over right foot.	Put position - body leaning to one side (backwards)
Lift - Hips drive forward, left leg starts bent then straightens, free arm high.	Lift - body turned too early, not enough hip turn/drive
Arm strike - right elbow high, hips push forward, chest pushes up, head faces up, the action is fast.	Arm strike - elbow low, hip turn too small, chest faces forwards (not up), whole action is slow
Release - head looks up, chest pushes out, hips are forward, left leg straight and braced, shot released at a 41 degree angle.	Release - head to the side, chest low, hips turn forward after the release, shot released too flat

Rule infringements

All rules are kept - shot stays in contact with the neck until pushed forward, the whole action takes place in the circle, the performer exits from the rear of the circle.

Planning for improvement – Components of skill-related fitness to improve

Strength - more explosive strength required - more muscular strength and speed training needed to increase the distance of the shot.

Agility - to effect a quick action maintaining a stable and controlled position.

Training principles to apply

Specificity - work at performer's level and develop skills for shot put.

Overload - training demands require body to adapt and so improve performance - safe levels are set for each performer.

Progression - as programme continues individual is re-tested - gradual changes made to frequency, intensity and time for new programme.

Weight training - improve explosive power by lifting heavy weights quickly, concentrating on upper body and leg strength to gradually increase strength and speed.

Use 'weight training repetitions' for a beginner or use 'pyramid sets' for experienced performer.

After three weeks re-measure/test strength – alter the weights accordingly.

Practices to help improvement (isolating part of the action)

Unsteady shift backwards

Balance - practise the following actions starting slowly and gradually building up the pace:
i) Without the shot   ii) With shot lightweight substitute   iii) With the correctly weighted shot

1 Isolated kick back

a) Adopt stance and balance on one leg
b) Swing leg and shift backwards three times in a row

2 Single kick back to foot plant

a) Swing leg
b) Swing leg and shift backwards
c) Shift backwards and plant on to other foot
Repetitive practice needs to be checked by the coach/teacher. The performer can use a self-check system but regular monitoring is required by the coach/teacher.

Execution of the release too slow

Explosive power -

a) Follow chosen weight training programme (lifting heavy weights a few times).
b) Isolate arm extension. Perform in a correct and controlled way, starting slowly, then gradually increasing pace.
c) Link arm action with chest extension part of the action, again gradually building up pace.

Shot drops too early

Reinforce correct angle of release – 41 degrees.
Emphasise extension and high finish of the arm.
Strength and speed training may help correct the fault.

Tactics to aid improvement

In competition - secure first throw as a counting attempt then go for all-out distance.

OCR Analysis Form – Athletics – Shot put

Candidate Sam Smith	**Date** 20/03/04	**Analysis attempt** First	**Own/others' performance**
Activity Shot put	**Playing position** R/handed	**Experience** 4 years	**Conditions** Dry and clear

Identified skills needed for the activity –

Explosive muscular strength (anaerobic fitness) combined with speed to produce:

Power - pushing the shot as far as is possible for that performer.

Balance - giving a stable base from which to complete the action and put the shot.

Agility - being able to shift the body weight backwards at pace, change direction and keep body controlled.

Speed - needed in the shift/glide and arm strike action.

Strengths in the performance

1 Three fingers behind with thumb and little finger supporting underneath.

2 Correct stance in balance position - shoulders square, right foot straight, free leg balancing body and flexed ('T' position).

To improve strengths

1 Training principles - Correct grip

Specificity

Methods   Repeat practice

Watch video to check procedure

Practices   Continue with the correct grip, systematically going through checkpoints (remember 'clean palm, dirty neck').

Increase the competitive situations so that the correct grip can still be adopted under pressure.

Write down the order of adopting the correct grip in diary form. This can start a performance diary of your activity.

---

2 Training principles - Correct stance in balanced position.

Frequency - increase the number of sessions per week.

Methods   Self-check/coach/teacher check repetitive practice.

Practices   Continue with the correct stance: elbow out and away from body, shoulders square.

Increase the competitive situations so that the stance can still be adopted under pressure.

Combine the beginning stance smoothly with the crouch.

Weaknesses in the performance	Reasons for the weaknesses
1 Unsteady shift backwards.	1 Poor balance - muscle not trained enough so more practice needed.
2 Slow arm action.	2 No appreciation of the correct action.
3 Shot drops too early resulting in short distance attempt.	3 Shot released not at 41 degrees angle/strength-related fault.

How to correct the weaknesses

1 Training principles

- Unsteady shift backwards

Specificity - develop skills at performer's level - focus on the backwards movement.

Progression - as programme continues, gradually increase the pace (intensity).

Methods Self/coach/teacher to check practice = 'repetitive practice' isolating the action.

Practices 1 Ten repetitions of three kick backs in a row.

2 Balance - practise the following actions starting slowly and gradually building up the pace i) without the shot ii) with shot lightweight substitute ('softball') iii) with the correctly weighted shot.

a) Adopt correct stance and balance on one leg add - b) Swing leg like a pendulum, keeping balanced add -
c) Swing leg and shift backwards off the heel add - d) Shift backwards and plant on to other foot keeping head steady and facing back of circle.

If the performer uses a 'self-check' system, regular monitoring is required by coach/teacher.

2 Training principles

- Slow arm action

Specificity - work at safe levels for performer concentrating on technique.

Overload - gradually increase the load to be put (to over the shot weight) - use the resistance to increase muscle strength.

Progression - after 3 weeks re-test - gradual changes made to frequency, intensity and time of new programme.

Methods Weight training - (improve explosive power = lifting heavy weights quickly) concentrating on upper body/leg strength to gradually increase strength and speed.

Beginners = 'simple sets', experienced athlete = 'pyramid sets'.

Practices a) Isolate arm extension. Perform in correct and controlled way, starting slowly, then gradually increasing pace.

b) Link arm and chest extension part of action, gradually building up the pace.

Continually monitor changes to muscle strength and the distances thrown.

3 Training principles

- Shot drops too early

Specificity - reinforce correct angle of release - 41 degrees and arm finishing high.

Progression - gradually increase intensity i.e. height of the suspended ball so it is more demanding to succeed.

Methods Self-check practice, coach/teacher check.

Strength and speed training may help correct the fault.

Practices Repeat skill, making sure technique shows arm at 41 degrees starting slowly.

Emphasise extension of the arm - repeat the action (without the shot) to reach for a target - when arm is correctly, fully extended they can touch an object set for their height (use a practice volleyball suspended from a netball post).

Record of discussions on findings

Gradually building up the skills for the 'shift' took a lot of concentration but worked.

It was difficult to keep to my strength-training programme; professional athletes must work very hard.

Setting up the volleyball was time-consuming, but it did make me reach and extend my arm. The coach also decided to time how long it took me, which was fun.

APPLYING KNOWLEDGE, PRINCIPLES, METHODS AND TRAINING PRACTICES

> Gather as much information as you can about your sport from different sources

Applying knowledge

Your knowledge of the event will come from different sources – personal experience, knowledge of the coaching points from teacher/coach/reference material, experience of watching peers perform and experience of watching top class performers in action on TV, video or live.

When assessing shot put, check the following:

Are the basics right?

- Is the direction of movement correct?
- Is the rhythm correct?

Possible reasons for poor performance:

- athlete does not understand the correct movement
- poor physical ability
- coordination is poor
- power applied incorrectly
- lack of concentration
- clothing not right for the event
- the conditions may affect the performance
- tactics and strategies wrong for the situation.

Planning for improvement

When planning an exercise programme, the order below shows a possible train of thought that could be followed:

- identify the areas needed to improve by comparing the action with the perfect model
- isolate the part of the action needing improvement
- recognise the skill-related fitness involved
- recognise the muscles involved
- recognise the health-related factors involved
- choose the training methods that can be adapted to the event (consult the performer as there may be preferences which will make training more fun)
- test and measure the ability of the performer
- draw up your six-week plan.

Testing and measuring the skills

When testing and measuring the performer, it is important to focus on the skills and abilities needed for the particular activity. For a person to be successful in the shot put, one of the areas they need to develop is explosive strength. This is a combination of strength and speed which when combined makes a powerful action, which in turn can increase the distance the shot put travels. A test that can measure explosive strength is the **vertical jump test**. This concentrates on assessing the strength of the lower body.

Explosive strength – The vertical jump test

Equipment needed:

- indoor area
- measuring tape
- chalk
- recorder and recording sheet.

To conduct the test:

1 The athlete stands sideways to the wall.

2 With feet flat on the floor, athlete reaches with their arm nearest to the wall.

3 The height where the stretched fingers reach is measured.

4 Standing slightly away from the wall (for safety), the athlete jumps vertically as high as possible, using arms and legs for maximum strength.

5 They touch the wall at the highest point possible (by chalking the fingers, a clear mark is left to measure).

6 The distance between the two measures is recorded.

7 The athlete has three attempts.

Vertical jump test results table

Rating	Male (cm)	Female (cm)
excellent	>70	>60
very good	61–70	51–60
above average	51–60	41–50
average	41–50	31–40
below average	31–40	21–30
poor	21–30	11–20
very poor	<21	<11

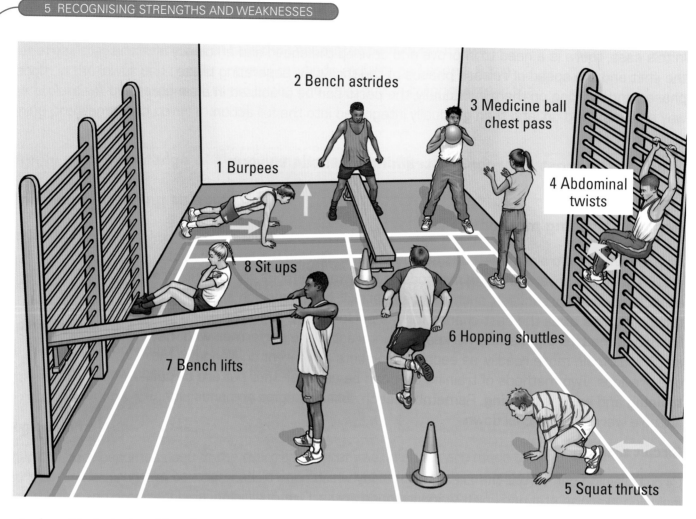

▲ *A possible circuit adapted for a shot put athlete.*

▼ *A six-week training programme*

The circuit length can vary between six and ten stations. It is advisable to work between 20–30 seconds at each station, with a 30-second rest period between each station. Complete the whole circuit, gradually building up to three to five times (sets) with a recovery period between each set of three minutes. Regular testing is necessary to measure progress and it may be necessary to increase the intensity of the circuit. This can be done every four weeks.

Changing the numbers of stations; time of exercise; sets and repetitions can all modify the intensity. The following table is an example of how the sessions can vary.

Week			
1	Test and measure performer and plan programme from findings		
	Intensity	Time at each station	Number of sets
2	65% of maximum	30 seconds	2
3	75% of maximum	20 seconds	3
4	75% of maximum	25 seconds	3
5	80% of maximum	20 seconds	2
6	Re-test and plan new programme from findings		

Weight training

This method is the most widely used for increasing strength. It involves lifting weights according to the performer's ability, repeating the lift a number of times (repetitions) and repeating the decided number of lifts again (sets).

Muscles will become stronger by gradually increasing the intensity by:

- adding more weight (resistance)
- increasing the number of repetitions
- increasing the number of sets
- reducing the recovery time (intensity).

Before any weight training is undertaken, the performer is tested to determine how strong they are and find out what their maximum lift capacity is. The findings can be worked out as a percentage and applied to the training programme.

The exercises used should match the demands of the shot put event and so the muscles specifically needed are identified and exercised accordingly. The strength of the performer should be re-tested after four to six weeks and the programme readjusted depending on the results.

Exercises appropriate to the shot put would include:

- Shoulder press
- Chest press
- Lateral pull down
- Lower back extension
- Triceps press
- Calf raises
- Bicep curls
- Leg curls
- Leg extensions

Weight training sessions can be adapted to the experience and needs of the performer. The weights lifted are always dependent on the performer's ability.

Simple sets

The performer lifts weights that are 70 per cent of the maximum weight they are able to lift. Eight repetitions of the exercise are made. This is repeated three times (three sets). Simple sets are suitable for the novice lifter.

Week 4 Training 3

   a) Circuit training

   b) Weight training

   c) Conditioning*

   d) General game

Week 5 Training 4

   a) Circuit training

   b) Weight training

   c) Technique combining skills in the throw

   d) General game

Week 6 Re-test and measure: leg strength, upper body strength and speed. Set new programme from the findings.

*Conditioning

Conditioning exercises target specific muscle groups. The following are examples for leg and upper body exercises:

Legs	Upper body
bounding	sit-ups
hopping	back arches
single leg squats	reverse curl
side hopping over a six inch hurdle	
multi-gym exercises – leg press, standing heel raises, half squats	

Timescale for a year leading up to a top class competition

The time span leading up to a competition controls the shape of the plan. It is important to peak at the time of the competition and use the periods in between to reduce the stress levels so that overuse injuries do not occur. Each part of the year plays a specific role in the development of the athlete. Some phases are more demanding than others and some specifically allow the athlete to reduce the training and recover the body.

Within the training programme, attention will be given to all aspects of the event, both physical and mental. Each session should vary in order to keep the athlete mentally stimulated, interested and positive. This can be achieved by mixing up conditioning, skill, technique and general training with mental preparation for the competition.

The training year for an athlete begins around October, when work starts on the general fitness of the athlete. The start of phase one is determined by the timings of the competitions, with training building up to each competition.

The year plan for an athlete competing in the outdoor season competitions can look like this:

A year plan for the throw athlete

Phase 1 (sixteen weeks)

November–December–January–February

Aim – General fitness development and basic technique

Training three times per week:

a) isolating parts of the throw
b) strength, mobility and coordination exercises
c) strength work using circuit and weight training
d) conditioning legs and upper body.

Phase 2 (eight weeks)

February–March

Aim – The development of specific fitness and advanced skills

Training three times per week:

a) technique training with more intensity
b) specific strength, mobility and coordination work
c) general strength work with circuit and weight training.

Phase 6 (four weeks)

September–October

Aim – Recovery and planning for the following season.

General fitness levels maintained through a moderate fitness training programme.

Phase 3 (eight weeks)

April–May

Aim – Experience of competition and opportunity to qualify for main events

Training three times per week:

a) technique work
b) full throw practice using modified weighted shot
c) exercises concentrating on speed
d) general strength work with circuit and weight training.

Phase 5 (eight weeks)

July–August

Aim – Competition, experience and reaching set targets

Training three times per week:

a) technique practices
b) general strength work with circuit and weight training
c) full throw practice using same or lighter weighted shot
d) specific exercises for speed
e) competition.

Phase 4 (eight weeks)

June–July

Aim –Work on technique in preparation for the main event

Training three times per week:

a) technique training with increased intensity
b) general strength work with circuit and weight training
c) specific exercises for strength, mobility and coordination.

5 ▶ FOOTBALL EXAMPLE

When young players first start to play football they will rely on natural ability to do the best they can. To improve and progress further, particular components of skill-related fitness, health-related fitness and personal qualities need to be developed. By concentrating on these areas during training, a performer has the best chance to reach his or her potential in a game. Below are some of the areas a football player will need to work on to improve their play.

> **Know what makes up your chosen sport**

What makes a successful football player?

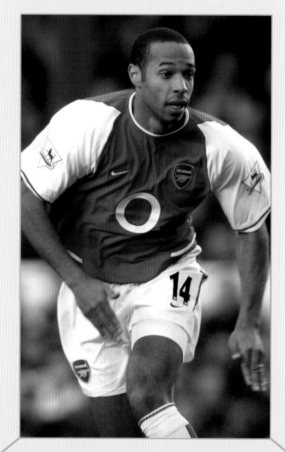

Skill-related fitness

- Agility – to out-manoeuvre opponents
- Speed – to move fast to avoid opponent/to mark opponent
- Power – to combine strength and speed together for long kicks/shooting
- Reaction time – to respond to opponents' movements or a quick passage of play

Health-related fitness

- Muscular endurance – to maintain high-skill levels throughout the game
- Flexibility – joints able to move into extreme positions without injury
- Muscular strength – to compete physically with other players and produce powerful shots
- Body composition – medium to large frame with muscle and little or no fat

Personal qualities

- Competitiveness
- Determination
- Good under pressure
- Contributor to team play
- Confidence

The perfect model

Footballers need many skills and qualities to be successful. A midfield player needs to link the defence and the attack. This requires both aerobic and anaerobic fitness. They have to be good at tracking back to mark a player and tackle for the ball. Midfielders also need to be accurate passers, often starting the attack with a penetrating pass. The long pass is often used by midfield players. This pass can often split the defence and be the start of an attacking move for players running off the ball in the attacking third of the pitch.

▲ *A time-lapsed illustration of a long pass.*

Know how the action is made up of small parts

Breaking down the action

When analysing the skill, be mindful of the different phases making up the action:

The approach – moving to collect the ball or pushing it into a space from where it is best to kick. Approach the ball from the side.

Base – position of the standing foot in relation to the ball and the distribution of weight over this base, maintaining stability.

Preparation – kicking leg swings back, standing leg flexes, arm on the non-kicking side held out to help balance the body.

Head position – head up with eyes looking at the ball.

Body position – torso is kept upright and leaning slightly back.

Contact – with the instep of the kicking foot.

Follow through – kicking leg sweeps through beyond the ball.

Recovery – balance and stance recovered quickly in order to reposition on the field according to the outcome of the pass.

Know the building blocks for the action

Building up the action

The parts of the whole action can be split up and trained individually. For the novice player, the following order may be used:

- the singular parts can be practised on their own
- link two skills together
- add a series of skills together
- add pace to the skills.

For the better performer, once the weakness in the action has been identified, that particular part can be focused on and singled out for concentrated attention in a similar way as for the novice.

A long pass can be built up using the following stages:

1 Use the instep to kick the ball into the air (kick-ups)

2 From a stationary position use the instep to kick the ball to a target

3 Add the approach from the side

4 Concentrate on achieving a stable base

5 Check the shape of the body

6 Add the follow through

The degree of difficulty can be increased by:

- working on your own
- having a passive opponent
- having an active opponent.

▲ *Kieron Dyer practises specific skills during training.*

Adapt a warm-up to your chosen sport

Suitable warm-up

As with all sports it is important to warm up prior to training or a game. The whole body should be warmed up aerobically first, followed by stretching exercises, using the muscles involved in the action of the activity, including: quadriceps, hamstrings, gluteals, abdominals, latissimus dorsi, pectorals, deltoids, biceps and triceps. Flexibility exercises are then completed in order to get the joints moving, and after these, more skills-based work links the general and specific action. Lastly, when the body is ready, more intense work can be attempted, for example, sprints. Remember that injury may occur if strenuous actions are attempted too early.

Psychologically, the warm-up will focus the mind of the performer and will help him or her prepare mentally for the game.

In brief, this is the order a warm-up should take:

Aerobic phase (5–10 minutes) – jogging or sidestepping to increase body temperature.

Flexibility phase (5–10 minutes) – **static stretches** to reduce muscle stiffness.

Stretch phase (5–10 minutes) – **dynamic (moving) stretches** to reduce muscle stiffness.

STATIC STRETCHES

▲ *Jogging and sidestepping can be used in the aerobic phase of the warm-up.*

Quadriceps Stretch

Arm out for balance (or place hand on wall) bend one leg behind and pull ankle towards buttocks

Side Leg Stretches

Stand with feet apart and lunge to one side, bending the forward knee while keeping the trailing leg straight

Sitting Leg Stretches

Legs straddled, bend at hips and reach forward

▲ *Flexibility exercises help to loosen the muscles around the joint.*

DYNAMIC STRETCHES

Leg Stretches

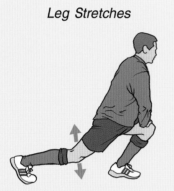

Gently raise and lower, stretching at the groin

Groin Stretches

Knees lift and lower, stretching at the groin

Hip Rotation

Standing on one leg lift knee and make large circles

Waist Twists

On one leg - arms twist to right - right leg lifts and crosses to the opposite side

Different teachers and coaches use different types of stretches. Before designing your programme check which type your teacher would prefer you to use.

AVOID ANY POSITION OF DISCOMFORT!

◀ *Flexing, relaxing, swinging, lifting, lowering and rotating body parts make up this phase.*

Skill phase (10-15 minutes) – specific drills for the sport such as passing, give and go or jumping to head the ball.

Increased intensity phase (2 minutes) – working on technique with greater intensity, imitating the action used in the event now performed at speed.

▲ *Real Madrid players practise sprinting before kick off.*

Cool down

5-10 minutes jogging or walking:

- helps to gradually decrease body temperature
- removes waste from the body.

5-10 minutes **static stretching**:

- decreases body temperature
- allows the muscles to relax
- helps prevent **DOMS** (delayed onset muscle soreness)
- reduces the chance of dizziness and fainting as it stops 'blood pooling' and reduces the level of adrenalin in the blood.

ANALYSIS EXAMPLE

The next section of work concentrates on how a candidate could go about analysing a football player in action. The scenario for the activity imitates what a student may observe whilst watching a performance. There then follows three examples of responses given for each of the following exam boards – AQA, Edexcel and OCR.

Scenario for the football example

The performer plays in the left midfield position and shows good aerobic fitness whilst keeping form throughout the game. He is willing to track back and move forward according to the play. He shows good speed from a standing start and can mark and tackle the opposition successfully. When in possession of the ball, the player likes to take members of the opposite team on, but sometimes can be dispossessed of the ball. He could make better use of the long pass to set up the attack. His game would improve if he looked up earlier and released a long pass sooner to penetrate the opposition's defence.

The following pages are responses made to the above scenario and give examples that could be used for each exam board (AQA, Edexcel and OCR). The layout and wording of the analysis sheets make every attempt to include all of the criteria stated in the examination specification. Every attempt has been made to use the terminology for that board.

AOA Analysis of Performance Form – Football

Candidate	Paul Perkins	Date	20/03/04	Analysis attempt	First	Own / others performance	
Activity	Football	Playing position	Left-midfield	Experience	5 years	Playing conditions	Dry, clear day

Analysis of performance

Comments

1. **Strength 1**   Links the defence with the attack and understands the need to track back after an attack.

2. **Strength 2**   Good close dribbling skills and has the confidence to take on an opponent.

3. **Weakness 1**   Sometimes tries to take on too many defenders.

4. **Weakness 2**   Could use the long ball more to split the defence.

Skill-related fitness needed

Agility - to change direction quickly whilst controlling the ball.

Speed - ability to quickly run into a space and/or keep up with an opponent in defence.

Power - to combine strength and speed to make an effective pass.

Understanding the activity

Dribble:

Using the body swerve   Ball on right foot   Dip left shoulder
Start to transfer the body weight as if going to the left then lean to the right transferring body weight
Push off with left leg to accelerate to the right

Long pass:

Approach the ball slightly from the side
Place standing foot a little in front of the ball with leg bent
Head up but with eyes looking at the ball
Torso upright
Opposite arm to kicking foot held out to balance the body
Kicking foot sweeps forward towards the ball
Weight slightly back
Contact with the ball made with the instep to give control and accuracy
The follow through is a long and smooth action

Improving performance

Nature/cause of strength/weakness

1. Keep working on anaerobic and aerobic fitness by using Fartlek training.

2. Attempt to perform dribbling techniques at a quicker pace without losing control of the ball.

3. Refine dribbling skills by successfully taking on a defender and finishing with an accurate pass before losing possession.

4. Learn how and when to make use of the long ball successfully in the game.

Analysis of Performance for GCSE PE

Targets for progress	Measuring	Monitoring
Understanding when to release the ball in order to keep possession for the team.	Dribbling and wall pass practice Score 2 points each for: - successful dribble - successful pass to player - controlling ball back from feeder - accurate long pass to target - when all four elements are put together.	Record each week's attempts/score and compare at the end of the three weeks. Work on weakest areas.
Play the long ball successfully.	Progressive long pass practice: For each attempt, check technique using check off list - two points for each correct technique and the success of the pass: a) Receive the ball - dribble - i: to a large target ii: medium target b) Repeat a) plus - passive defence - medium target c) Active defence - to a player	Record the results and compare and feed back after each session. Have twenty attempts at the practice, once every week, for three weeks.

Corrective measures

Practice set up

Dribbling:
1 Dribble with head up using peripheral vision to check the ball's position.
Practice - dribble and be able to tell how many fingers the coach is holding up.

2 Pass to an open player
Practice - dribble and on the signal of the team mate be able to adjust and deliver the pass quickly and accurately.

3 Use the body swerve to avoid opposition:
- if ball on right foot, dip left shoulder
- start to transfer body weight as if going to the left
- then quickly lean to the right transferring body weight
- push off with left leg to accelerate to the right.

For the long pass check the following coaching points for accuracy:
Check the angle of approach to the ball is to the side.
The standing foot should be slightly in front of the ball with leg bent.
Head held up but eyes looking at the ball.
Torso upright.
Arms used to balance the body - opposite arm to kicking foot should be held out as a counter balance.
Kicking foot sweeps forward towards the ball.
Weight slightly back.
Contact with the ball made with the instep to give control and accuracy.
The follow through is a long and smooth action.

5 RECOGNISING STRENGTHS AND WEAKNESSES 67

Edexcel Analysis Form

Candidate Paul Perkins	Date 20/03/04	Analysis attempt First	Own/others' performance
Activity Football	Playing position L/Midfield	Experience 5 years	Conditions Dry, clear day

Observation

Links the defence with the attack and understands the need to track back after an attack.

Has good, close dribbling skills and is confident to take on an opponent, but can take on too many at times.

Could use the long ball earlier to avoid losing the ball.

How viewed

Live game

Live practice

Video

Photo

Time-lapsed photo

Analysis – Important components of health/skill-related fitness

Agility - change direction quickly, keeping balance whilst controlling the ball.

Speed - to out-run opposition.

Power - to play pass/shot with enough force to beat opposition.

Reaction time - to respond to opponents' movements/own team play.

Stamina - to keep working skilfully throughout the game.

Strength - ability to tackle/be tackled combined with speed producing power.

Understand the action of a perfect model

Evaluation

Dribble:

Keep head up to see play - peripheral vision to see ball.

Keep ball close to feet.

Make small and quick steps so there is less time for the ball to be away from the feet.

Use the body swerve to avoid the opposition:
- if ball on right foot, dip left shoulder
- start to transfer body weight as if going to the left
- then quickly lean to the right transferring body weight
- push off with left leg to accelerate to the right.

Long pass:

Coaching points for long pass

1 Approach the ball slightly from the side.
2 Place standing foot slightly in front of the ball with leg bent.
3 Head up but eyes looking at the ball.
4 Torso upright.
5 Opposite arm to kicking foot held out to balance the body.
6 Kicking foot sweeps forward towards the ball.
7 Weight slightly back.
8 Contact with ball made with the instep to give control and accuracy.
9 The follow through is a long and smooth action.

Dribble:

Dribbles with head down so unable to see the play.

Ball too far away from the feet.

Does not make enough attempts to dummy the opposition.

Long pass:

Approach - too straight.

Standing foot - too far behind the ball.

Head down.

Body leaning forward.

Arms try to balance the body.

Good swing by kicking foot.

Weight too far forward.

Contact made with instep.

Follow through restricted.

Rule infringements

To avoid 'offside' the timing of the long ball is important - the ball must be released whilst there are two players of the defending team goal side of the attacker.

Planning for improvement – Components of skill-related fitness to improve

Agility to change efficiently from dribbling to passing under pressure.

Power so pass can reach the target.

Training principles to apply

Specificity - work at performer's level and develop football skills.

Overload - training demands put body under stress so it adapts, progresses and becomes stronger - safe levels are set for each performer.

Progression - as programme continues, individual is retested - gradual changes made to frequency, intensity and time for new programme.

Practices to help improvement (isolating part of the action)

<u>Dribble and passing practice</u>

Isolate parts of the skill and develop - ball control, balance, agility and awareness of team mates - use a check-off list with coach/observer recording and reinforcing actions.

Gradually link components back together, gradually increasing the intensity of execution.

Build up confidence to use the skill by gradually increasing the intensity of defence - no marker/passive marker/active marker.

<u>The Long Pass</u>

Build up confidence by changing the intensity of the practice. Start easy and gradually become more difficult i.e.

1. Play the pass from i. stationary ball ii. slightly moving ball iii. from a dribble.
2. Gradually build up the speed of performance.
3. Increase the degree of defence from i. no opposition ii. passive opposition iii. active opposition.
Use a check-off list comparing the performer with recognised good technique.

Possible variations are:
a) Play pass to hit a large target (into a goal).
b) Increase the distance gradually.
c) Play the pass from a dribble.
d) Add a passive defence influencing the timing of the pass.
e) Reduce the size of the target.
f) Play the pass from different positions so the angle to the target changes.

Tactics to aid improvement

Getting the body between the ball and defender to stop a tackle.

Playing the early ball - needs the attackers to be running off the ball.

Aim the long pass to the area just in front of the six yard box so that a header can be made.

OCR Analysis Form – Football

Candidate Paul Perkins	**Date** 20/03/04	**Analysis attempt** First	**Own/others' performance**
Activity Football	**Playing position** L/midfield	**Experience** 5 years	**Conditions** Dry and clear

Identified skills needed for the activity –

Agility - change direction quickly and keep balance whilst controlling the ball.

Speed - ability to quickly run into a space and/or keep up with an opponent in defence.

Power - combine strength and speed to play pass/shot with enough force to play effective pass to beat opposition.

Reaction time - to respond to opponents' movements/own team play.

Strengths in the performance

1 Links the defence with the attack and understands the need to track back after an attack.

2 Good close dribbling skills and has the confidence to take on an opponent.

To improve strengths

1 Training principles Improve anaerobic/aerobic capacity to adapt better to the changes in pace in the game.

Methods
Fartlek Training
Uses different distances, speed, times and terrain (hilly area, beach, forest) in the session.

Practices
Warm-up   Sprint for 10 seconds on flat   Jog on flat for 4 minutes   Sprint for 10 seconds uphill
Jog/walk downhill onto flat for 3 minutes   Run 150m on flat   Jog for 5 minutes on flat   Sprint 80m
uphill   Jog for 6 minutes downhill onto flat   Sprint 20m uphill   Jog downhill for 5 minutes onto flat
Sprint 10 seconds on flat   Jog/run downhill for 4 minutes on flat   Sprint 10 seconds uphill   Jog/run for
3 minutes downhill onto flat   Cool down

2 Training principles Practice for close dribbling skills

Methods   Control ball coming from different angles and then dribble.

Practices
a) Receive ball with back to goal, turn and dribble.
b) Receive an oncoming ball from the left.
c) Receive an oncoming ball from the right.
d) Control ball on chest and dribble.

Weaknesses in the performance	**Reasons for the weaknesses**
1 Sometimes tries to take on too many defenders.	1 Fails to see the easy pass to avoid being dispossessed.
2 When to hold up the ball and when to play a pass.	2 Unaware of the support play around.
3 Could use the long ball more to split the defence.	3 Lacks consistency and confidence with the long pass so uses it rarely.

How to correct the weaknesses

1 Training principles

Understanding when to release the ball, in order to keep possession for the team.

Specificity

Methods Isolate parts of the skill and develop - ball control, balance, agility and awareness of team mates - use a check-off list with coach/observer recording and reinforcing actions.
Gradually link components back together, gradually increasing the intensity of execution.

Practices Dribbling and wall pass practice
Score 2 points each for: - successful dribble - successful pass to player - controlling ball back from feeder
- accurate pass to team mate - when all four elements are put together.
Perform the skills with increasing levels of opposition to build up confidence.

Record each week's attempts/score and compare at the end of the three weeks. Work on weakest areas.

---

2 Training principles

When to hold up the ball and play a pass.

Specificity

Methods Practice to improve the understanding of when to stop the dribble and play a pass.

Practices Triangular pass
a) Dribble the ball and stop - keeping the head up to see the play.
b) Repeat a) plus - from the stop, turn (practice using both sides).
c) After the turn, play the pass to the open player.

Player must:
Keep ball close   Keep head up   Watch for team mate's movement.

---

3 Training principles

Could use long ball more to split the defence.   Specificity

Methods a) Check the skill by comparing the performance with a check-off list of recognised good technique.
Play the pass from - i. stationary ball ii. slightly moving ball iii. from a dribble.

Set up a practice situation to build up confidence by gradually increasing the intensity needed - e.g. speed of play, level of opposition and distance to pass.

Practices a) Play pass to hit a large target (into goal).   b) Increase the distance gradually.   c) Play the pass from a dribble.
d) Add a passive defence influencing the timing of the pass.   e) Reduce the size of the target.   f) Play the pass from different positions so the angle to the target changes.   g) Increase the level of defence.

Record of discussions on findings

Practising dribbling and turning gave me more skills to avoid being tackled.

By building up my speed in passing, I am able to use the wall pass more effectively and keep possession for my team.

I understand how the long pass can split a defence and how playing that pass just short of the six yard box puts the defence under most pressure.

APPLYING KNOWLEDGE, PRINCIPLES, METHODS AND TRAINING PRACTICES

Gather as much information as you can about your sport from different sources

Applying knowledge

Your knowledge of the event will come from different sources – personal experience, knowledge of the coaching points from teacher/coach/reference material, experience of watching peers perform and experience of watching top class performers in action on TV, video or live.

When assessing football, check the following:

External influences

Will the conditions affect the performance?

Is the competition of equal strength?

Are the basics right?

Is the player performing the skill in a controlled way?

Is the head in the right position?

Is the player balanced?

Is the body in the right position for the skill?

Is there follow through to the skill?

Do the skills work?

Is the preparation for the skill correct?

Is contact with the ball made in the right place?

Is the weight distributed correctly over the base?

Possible reasons for poor performance:

- performer does not understand the correct movement
- poor physical ability
- coordination is poor
- power applied incorrectly
- lack of concentration
- clothing not right for the event
- the conditions may affect the performance
- tactics and strategies wrong for the situation. (Strategies are the plan – tactics are how they are put into action.)

Planning for improvement

When planning an exercise programme, the order below shows a possible train of thought that could be followed:

- identify the areas needed to improve by comparing the action with the perfect model
- isolate the part of the action needing improvement
- recognise the skill-related fitness involved
- recognise the muscles involved
- recognise the health-related factors involved
- choose the training methods that can be adapted to the event (Consult the performer as there may be preferences which will make training more fun.)
- test and measure the ability of the performer
- draw up your six-week plan.

Testing and measuring the skills

When testing and measuring the performer, it is important to focus on the skills and abilities needed for the particular activity. To be a successful football player, you need to develop skills like: explosive strength, agility and stamina.

Explosive strength is a combination of strength and speed which makes a single action powerful. Power makes it possible to send passes further and faster, making them much more difficult for defences to either reach or stop.

Each skill has a test that can assess the ability of the performer. The **vertical jump test** can measure explosive strength of the lower body; agility can be tested by the **Illinois agility test**; and the **bleep test** measures stamina.

A top class player will be tested in all these areas and have built-in components in the training programme to cover them all.

Stamina – The Bleep Test

This test assesses the strength and efficiency of the heart and lungs. Good cardiovascular endurance will help a player to work hard throughout the game without losing breath or lowering performance.

Equipment needed:

- 20m length course set out between cones
- four cones
- tape or CD of the test
- cassette or CD player
- recorder and recording sheet

To conduct the test:

1 Athletes listen to the tape or the CD.

2 The athletes run to the cone and return only on the bleep.

3 If a player fails to reach the cone on the bleep twice in a row, then they are out.

4 The level they reached at that point is recorded as 'their level'.

> **Apply your knowledge of the principles of training**

Principles of training to apply

Overload

To improve the performer's condition, the performer must train the body harder than usual, without risking injury. As the body becomes used to the stresses of the exercises in the programme, then the load is gradually increased. This can be done by gradually increasing some or all of the following:

- frequency
- intensity
- duration (time) spent on the exercises.

Bleep test results table

Level	Shuttles	VO$_2$ max
4	9	25.5
5	9	32.9
6	10	36.4
7	10	39.9
8	10	43.3
9	11	46.8
10	11	50.2
11	12	53.7
12	12	57.1
13	13	74.4
14	13	64
15	13	67.5
16	14	70.9
17	14	74.4
18	15	77.9
19	15	81.3
20	15	84.8

▲ Cardiovascular endurance is tested by 'The Bleep Test'.

Progression

When the body becomes used to the exercise programme, changes are made to it so that further progress can be made (this is called **systematic programming**). Once the training programme is under way and regular sessions are completed each week, the body of the performer will adapt to the stress levels.

There will come a time when the original programme does not work the performer hard enough, and so has no effect. At this stage, the stresses of the programme need to be increased. The performer is tested again and changes to the programme can be made by gradually increasing the frequency, intensity and duration (time) spent on the exercise.

Specificity

When applying the principle of specificity to football, the coach should be mindful of the following:

- the technical exercises and practices used should copy the actual movements of the body in specific football actions
- the exercises should be performed at the speed required in the actual match for it to be useful to the performer.

Interval training adapts well to football. The skills used in the training should be those that closely relate to the skills used in the game. These are repeated to make up a complete set and then several sets may make up a session. When using this method, it is also important to apply the principle of specificity – the actions must not only resemble those used in the game, but must also be performed at a speed equivalent to that needed in the game.

> **Adapt the most appropriate training methods to your chosen sport**

Applying training methods

An assortment of training methods can be used to develop the body for football. By adapting several training methods to the event, a focus can be put on all aspects needed for success, such as: areas of skill, body condition and technique. This gives the best chance for the performer to progress. Varying the focus and the training method will keep the interest of the performer, who may as a result train more readily, as each session sets a different challenge to the one previous. Two of the methods of training that can be used for football are **circuit training** and **Fartlek training**. Remember, each session begins and ends with a suitable warm-up and cool down.

Circuit training

Circuit training can target the areas of the body which need to be improved by including exercise stations solely working those areas. Circuit training is an excellent way of increasing strength and providing clearly defined challenges. This method can also bring a competitive edge to the training, as the performer knows the targets he or she has to achieve. Some of the skills used in football can be adapted and included as one of the station's exercises. This adds variety to the training and allows the opportunity of training with the rest of the team.

The footballer can use the circuit to concentrate on particular skills, general fitness or even concentrate on improving leg strength. The performer should be tested to see what their maximum number of repetitions in the allotted time is at each station and the programme based around these findings.

Below is an example of a circuit including exercises suitable for the footballer.

1 Step-ups (legs)

2 Wall pass (legs)

3 Throw on (arms and abdominals)

9 Sit-ups (abdominals)

8 Target passing (legs)

4 Bench astrides (legs)

7 Dribbling (legs)

5 Kick-ups (legs)

6 Heading (head and neck)

▲ *A possible circuit adapted for football.*

The circuit length can vary between six and ten stations. It is advisable to work between 20–30 seconds at each station with a 30-second rest period between each station. Complete the whole circuit, gradually building up to three to five times (sets) with a recovery period between each set of three minutes. Regular testing is necessary to measure the progress and it may be necessary to increase the intensity of the circuit. This can be done every four weeks.

Changing the numbers of stations; time of exercise; sets and repetitions can modify the intensity. The following table is an example of how the sessions can vary.

A six-week training programme

Week			
1	Test and measure performer and plan the programme from findings		
	Intensity	**Time at each station**	**Number of sets**
2	65% of maximum	30 seconds	2
3	75% of maximum	20 seconds	3
4	75% of maximum	25 seconds	3
5	80% of maximum	20 seconds	2
6	Re-test and plan new programme from findings		

Fartlek Training

A football player needs both aerobic and anaerobic respiration fitness. Aerobic strength will provide the stamina to keep working throughout the game and the anaerobic fitness will allow short, sharp bursts of maximum effort. Fartlek training provides work rates at both these levels.

By incorporating this training method into the programme, the coach adds variety for the players by providing a chance to work in a different environment than the usual training ground.

Remember each training session starts and ends with a warm-up and cool down respectively.

Components of a possible Fartlek training session

Phase	Speed	Time/distance	Terrain
1	Sprint	10 seconds	Flat
2	Jog/run	5 minutes	Flat
3	Sprint	10 seconds	Uphill
4	Jog/walk	6 minutes	Downhill onto flat
5	Run	150 metres	Flat
6	Jog	5 minutes	Flat
7	Sprint	80 metres	Uphill
8	Jog	6 minutes	Downhill onto flat
9	Sprint	20 metres	Uphill
10	Jog	4 minutes	Downhill onto flat
11	Sprint	10 seconds	Flat
12	Jog/walk	4 minutes	Downhill onto flat
13	Sprint	10 seconds	Uphill
14	Jog/run	3 minutes	Downhill onto flat

> **Apply your knowledge of training practices to your chosen sport**

Applying training practices

When working on a personal exercise programme (**PEP**) for a performer, a good starting point is to know what the training is working towards. This will determine the most appropriate exercises, training methods and work rates to be applied.

Testing and measuring the performer's initial strength and ability is vital. It is from these findings that the correct level of exercise can be set. The right degree of intensity will help the performer to progress, but must not be too demanding, otherwise injury may occur.

If the programme is working towards a specific event, like a football match for instance, the programme should include exercises and skills relevant to that game. So an understanding and knowledge of the event and actions included should be taken into account and applied to the programme. This is the principle of specificity.

Wherever possible an understanding of the performer's training preferences should be adapted to the programme. They may prefer working on their own, in a group or even in a particular setting. This makes the training more interesting and enjoyable and will motivate the performer to work harder.

For the training to make a difference, three sessions should be completed per week, working over 60 per cent of the maximum level of intensity for greater than 20 minutes at a time.

Working at this frequency, intensity and duration (time), it may be that within four weeks' time, the performer's body will have adapted to the training. At this stage, a re-testing of the performer is necessary, so changes can be made to the programme and further progress can be made in the future.

Timescale for a six-week PEP

The following six-week plan focuses on strength, anaerobic and aerobic respiration skills and technique for an outfield football player. Each session starts with a warm-up and finishes with a cool down. The pattern of the programme includes circuit and Fartlek training, skill and technique work and a team game, giving variety and interest for the player.

Week 1 Test and measure: strength, stamina and speed.

Week 2 Training 1
 a) Circuit training
 b) Skill and technique
 c) Fartlek training
 d) General game

Week 3 Training 2
 a) Circuit training
 b) Skill and technique
 c) Fartlek training
 d) General game

Week 4 Training 3
 a) Circuit training
 b) Skill and technique
 c) Fartlek training
 d) General game

Week 5 Training 4
 a) Circuit training
 b) Skill and technique
 c) Fartlek training
 d) General game

Week 6 Re-test and measure: strength, stamina and speed. Set new programme from the findings.

▲ *Training at the correct levels is vital to performance.*

Timescale of the football year

The timing of the football season controls the shape of the training plan. It is important to peak for the season and then for particular cup matches that there might be. There may be times when players are rested for games and the strength of the squad becomes a factor for success. The coach will build in times when the intensity and method of training are varied so that overuse injuries do not occur. Each part of the year plays a specific role in the development of the player. Some phases are highly demanding, whereas other phases specifically reduce training and allow recovery of the body.

The perfect model

There are many skills required in netball that lead to effective play, each requiring specialised training. Shooting skills, if performed well, can boost the team's confidence as the players have worked hard to get the ball into the circle for the opportunity to add to their score. Both the goal attack and goal shooter are allowed to shoot. When taking a shot they will need to concentrate on the following phases of the action if they are to be successful.

▲ A time-lapsed illustration of a plain shot.

Know how the action is made up of small parts

Breaking down the action

When analysing the action be mindful of the different phases making up the whole action. The performer should remember that the shot could come after a run into the circle or a dodge from a confined space. The body must quickly adjust into a balanced position, the base should be steady, the best technique should be adopted, aim taken and the shot made – all within three seconds. The following outline breaks down the action for a plain standing shot:

Base

– feet set apart just enough to maintain balance
– the foot on the throwing arm side should be forward (this should be the landing foot to increase the distance between the defender).

Support

– ball held in both hands above the head
– dominant hand behind the ball
– other hand stabilising the ball to the side
– wrist of dominant hand is cocked
– ball supported by the base of the fingers.

Fingers spread

- middle finger in line with the target
- shooting arm at right angles at shoulder and elbow
- ball, eyes and target should all be in a line.

Aiming

- concentrate on the furthest part of the ring.

Preparation

- knees flex
- push up from legs through body.

Release

- ball directed up and high towards the target
- arm fully extends
- wrist 'snaps' on release
- fingers relax and move in a downward direction in a 'waving goodbye to the ball' action.

Result

- due to the action of the hand and fingers the ball travels with backspin
- the trajectory should be able to avoid the defence – reaching the post over the front of the ring
- a perfect result will see the ball cleanly through the ring
- if sent slightly too far the backspin will send the ball into the goal from the back of the ring
- player follows through towards the post
- any follow through must avoid contact with the defence.

▲ *England shooter, Alex Astle, takes a shot at goal against New Zealand.*

(Know the building blocks for the action)

Building up the action

1 **Footwork** – be able to take the ball from the air in any direction landing:

   a) on one foot after the other and adjust to post

   b) both feet at the same time and adjust to post

   c) balancing on one foot only (when catching the ball on the edge of the court).

2 Support of the ball with fingers spread – practise putting backspin on the ball by playing the ball:

   a) in the air

   b) against a wall at a high target.

3 Focus – when shooting, concentrate on the far rim of the ring and combine with the previous backspin practice to make a shot at goal.

4 Preparation – flexing the knees and extending up through the body without the ball, then with the ball but with no release of the ball yet.

5 Release – add release to the previous practice.

Combine all the practices together, finishing with a shot on goal:

a) passing the ball to self with no defence

b) passing ball to self with a passive defence to shoot over

c) passing ball to self with an active defender attempting to stop the shot

d) passing ball to self with an active defender attempting to stop the shot and another defender going for the rebound

e) follow the above phases with the shooter receiving the ball from open play.

Adapt a warm-up to your chosen sport

Suitable warm-up

All activities and sports need a suitable, thorough and appropriate warm-up. The intensity of the warm-up should start with low impact exercises and then gradually increase. The whole body should be warmed up aerobically first, followed by stretching exercises, using the muscles involved in the action of the activity, including: quadriceps, hamstrings, gluteals, abdominals, latissimus dorsi, pectorals, deltoids, biceps and triceps. Flexibility exercises are then completed. As striding, stretching and throwing over distance are a major part of the game, special attention is given to the joints of the lower body and the arms and shoulders. Skill work, followed by greater intensity exercises, completes the warm-up.

In brief, this is the order a warm-up should take:

Aerobic phase (5–10 minutes)

1 Jog freely around the court – on the whistle, change direction.

2 Jog freely around two courts – jump into the air when a line is reached.

3 Jog freely around the court – on the whistle, jump, land, step and stop.

4 Group divided into four teams each with different coloured bibs. On command, a colour is called out and that team tags the others. If tagged, they continue by hopping or skipping whilst the game continues until the next whistle change and a new tag team is chosen.

Flexibility phase (5–10 minutes) – **static stretches** to reduce muscle stiffness. This phase ensures the muscles around the joint are prepared for full extension.

▶ *Flexibility exercises help to loosen the muscles around the joint.*

Stretch phase (5–10 minutes) – **dynamic (moving) stretches** to reduce muscle stiffness. Areas for special attention are the muscles of:

a) the lower body – gastrocnemius, hamstrings, gluteals and abdominals

b) the torso – latissimus dorsi, pectorals and deltoids

c) upper body – biceps, triceps and trapezium.

▶ *Flexing, relaxing, swinging, lifting, lowering and rotating body parts make up this phase.*

Different teachers and coaches use different types of stretches. Before designing your programme check which type your teacher would prefer you to use.

AVOID ANY POSITION OF DISCOMFORT!

STATIC STRETCHES

Shoulder Stretch

Quadriceps Stretch

Hamstring Stretches

Arm reaches across chest and other arm applies pressure at the elbow to work shoulder

Arm out for balance (or place hand on wall) bend one leg behind and pull ankle towards buttocks

One leg straight out, body leans forward so hands can reach as far as possible (comfortably) down leg

DYNAMIC STRETCHES

Flexing/Relaxing

From sitting position tuck knees in flexing abdominals and relax

Lifting/Lowering

From the side lift and lower arms

Swinging

Swing arms forward and back

Rotating

Lift knees and rotate at hip

Skill phase (10–15 minutes) – specific drills for the sport; gradually the muscles are exercised closer to the manner needed in the game by incorporating the skills needed for play.

1 Passing drill

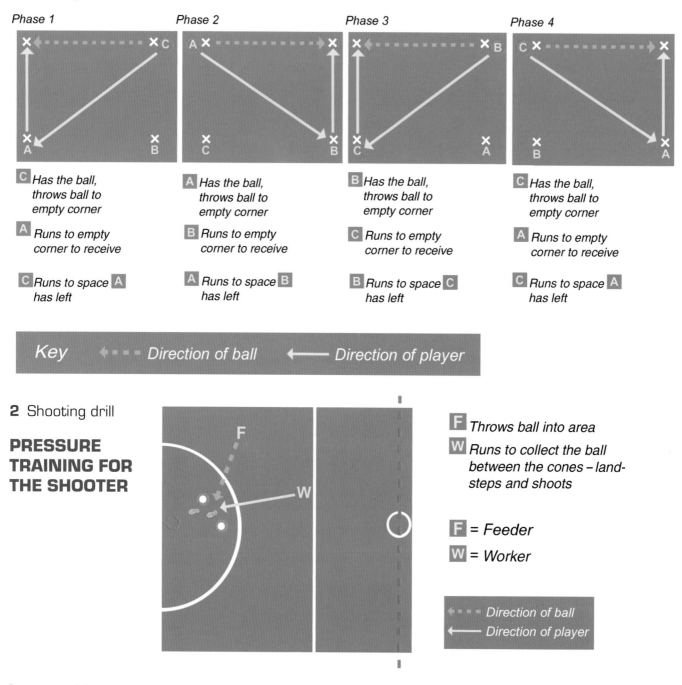

Phase 1

C Has the ball, throws ball to empty corner

A Runs to empty corner to receive

C Runs to space A has left

Phase 2

A Has the ball, throws ball to empty corner

B Runs to empty corner to receive

A Runs to space B has left

Phase 3

B Has the ball, throws ball to empty corner

C Runs to empty corner to receive

B Runs to space C has left

Phase 4

C Has the ball, throws ball to empty corner

A Runs to empty corner to receive

C Runs to space A has left

Key ◄---- Direction of ball ◄——— Direction of player

2 Shooting drill

PRESSURE TRAINING FOR THE SHOOTER

F Throws ball into area

W Runs to collect the ball between the cones – land-steps and shoots

F = Feeder
W = Worker

◄---- Direction of ball
◄——— Direction of player

Increased intensity phases (2 minutes) – increased intensity phases similar to the game. These involve sprints and modified games, such as a 4 v 4 mini game using one third of the court and the circle (see opposite page).

Remember an appropriate cool down to prevent following discomfort

4 v 4 MINI GAME ▶

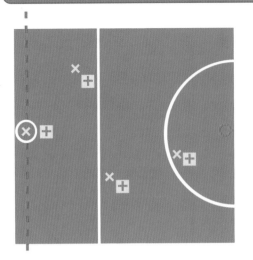

Cool down

5–10 minutes jogging or walking:

- helps to gradually decrease body temperature
- removes waste from the body.

5–10 minutes **static stretching**:

- decreases body temperature
- allows the muscles to relax
- helps prevent **DOMS** (delayed onset muscle soreness)
- reduces the chance of dizziness and fainting by stopping 'blood pooling' and reduces the level of adrenalin in the blood.

One team attacks goal to shoot (attackers) to score.
One team attacks area on line with centre circle (defenders) to score.
One defender and one attacker allowed in circle.
Attackers start with ball in centre circle.
After a goal by attackers, defenders restart with ball behind goal line.
After defenders have reached the correct area attackers restart from centre circle.

⊗ *= Attackers*
➕ *= Defenders*

ANALYSIS EXAMPLE

The next section of work concentrates on how a candidate could go about analysing a netball player in action. The scenario for the activity suggests what a student may observe whilst watching a performance. There then follows three examples of responses given for each of the following exam boards – AQA, Edexcel and OCR.

Scenario for the netball example

The goal attack is very mobile and supports play, moving the ball from defence to attack efficiently. Her chest passing is accurate and usually makes the target. She often receives the ball just inside the circle but her accuracy in shooting has only a fair success rate.

When she shoots, the ball is held out to one side and her stance is awkward, lacking sufficient balance to provide a steady base for the shot.

The following pages are responses made to the above scenario and give examples that could be used for each exam board (AQA, Edexcel and OCR). The layout and wording of the analysis sheets make every attempt to include all of the criteria stated in the examination specification. Every attempt has been made to use the terminology for that board.

AQA Analysis of Performance Form – Netball – Shooting

Candidate	Jade Jones	Date	20/03/04	Analysis attempt	First	Own / others performance	
Activity	Netball	Playing position	Goal Attack – right handed	Experience	5 years	Playing conditions	Dry, clear day

Analysis of performance

Comments

1. **Strength 1** — Good at finding space and supporting attacking and defensive play.

2. **Strength 2** — In circle, successful passing to goal shooter so the shot can be taken nearer the goal.

3. **Weakness 1** — only 50% of the shots are successful due to her attempting to shoot too far from goal.

4. **Weakness 2** — A common fault is that the shots fall too short of the target. Possible reasons – the ball is held too low and to the side of the body, and a poor whole body action results in a lack of power.

Skill-related fitness needed

Understanding the activity

Balance – For a steady position on one or two feet from which to shoot.

Speed – dodging opponent at pace to create space to receive the ball.

Coordination – passing and shooting accurately.

Reaction time – ability to jump for the ball after it rebounds off the goal post.

Agility – to change direction in confined spaces to receive ball successfully in a space without causing contact.

Power – to spring into the air to collect the ball.

Balance
Speed
Coordination
Reaction time
Agility
Power

Improving performance

Nature/cause of strength/weakness

1. Shows good agility – able to change direction quickly and keep balanced. Has 'quick feet' for dodging. Good aerobic ability working well in both thirds. Good anaerobic ability to move in short bursts from a standing start.

2. Passing is accurate, showing good technique and an understanding of both throwing the ball ahead of the player or directly to the player's hands. As her throwing action is quick, she responds well to signals from the GS.

3. Her success rate at shooting is poor because she does not allow the ball to be lined up with the target, plus the technique lacks full body movement and follow through with shooting arm.

4. Shots fall short due to the lack of good technique of the player and the distance of shot required.

Targets for progress	Measuring	Monitoring
Improve technique of the shooting action. Perform the shots complying with a check-off list of the correct technique. Look at a time-lapsed drawing of the action.	For each shot, tick off when the skill is performed: correct stance, ball position preparation, head/hand/ball and target in line, flexing of the knees, extension of the arm, follow through.	Video and watch performer's action to check improvements needed. Take 30 shots. Partner ticks off successful parts of the action (gives feedback). Re-video and make adjustments.
Increase success rate of shots attempted. Find optimum place to shoot from (where most successful). Set a target each week increasing by 15% for three weeks.	In the circle, set out markers at six different distances and angles from the post. Score one point for every successful shot (no defence). Keep a record of each success.	Have ten shots from each position. Repeat three times. Compare the results and work out which position gives the best success.

Corrective measures	Practice-set up

Improve shooting technique:

Check the following coaching points for accuracy:

Base - feet apart, weight evenly distributed, landing foot forward. A right-handed shooter should try to land on right foot.

Support of ball - ball held above head, fingers spread behind and underneath, wrist cocked, other hand stabilising to the side, elbow at right-angle.

Aiming - head/hand/ball and target in line, eyes focusing on furthest point of ring.

Preparation - flexing of the knees, then extending up through body ending with extension of arm.

Release - ball directed up and away from body, with a snap of the wrist ('wave goodbye to the ball') - this applies backspin to ball.

Follow through - in direction of goal with movement of the feet to follow up shot, being sure to avoid contact with defender.

Improve the success rate of shots:

Receive ball nearer optimum position for successful shot.

Hold position prior to moving to receive - allows movement to the favoured position.

Feint and dodge - base narrow, weight on balls of feet, evenly distributed, give smallest effective decoy feint, then push with furthest leg away from the feint, turning the body and indicating for the ball.

Finish receiving the ball in favoured position.

Edexcel Analysis of Performance Form – Netball – Shooting

Candidate Jade Jones	Date 20/03/04	Analysis attempt First	Own/others' performance
Activity Netball - shooting	Playing position Goal attack – r/handed	Experience 5 years	Conditions Dry, clear day

Observation

The player supports the attack and defence well. Passes effectively to shooter in circle.

Only 50% of shots are successful. Usual fault - shots fall short of the target. Possible reasons -

1. poor technique in ball support and whole body action.

2. Shots made too far from the target.

How viewed

Live game

Live practice

Video

Photo

Time lapsed photo

Analysis – Important components of health/skill-related fitness

Speed - outmanoeuvre opponent   Agility - manoeuvre quickly in confined spaces

Power - spring to catch ball   Balance - land from any direction keeping to footwork rules

Reaction - adjust quickly to opposition and turn over play   muscular strength - to help with power

Muscular endurance - work and concentrate for whole match   Flexibility - adopt extreme body positions without injury

Body composition - build for the position

Understand the action of a perfect model

Evaluation

Shooting:

Base - feet apart, weight evenly distributed, landing foot forward.

Support of ball - ball held above head, fingers spread, behind and underneath, wrist cocked, other hand stabilising to the side, elbow at right angle.

Aiming - head/hand/ball and target in line, eyes focused to furthest point of ring.

Preparation - flex knees, then extend up through body to the extension of the arm.

Release - ball directed up and away from body, with a snap of the wrist ('wave goodbye to the ball' applies backspin).

Follow through - in direction of goal with movement of feet to follow-up shot, being sure to avoid contact with the defender.

Receive ball at optimum position for successful shot:

- hold position prior to moving
- base narrow
- weight on balls of feet
- weight evenly distributed.

Feint - give smallest effective decoy feint and dodge away from finish area.

Dodge - then push with furthest leg away from the feint, turning the body and indicating for the ball.

Finish receiving the ball in favoured position.

Shooting:

Base - good

Support of ball - ball should be held higher above the head with wrist cocked.

Aiming - needs to line up hand/head/ball and target more accurately.

Preparation - knees need to flex with body extending during the action.

Release - arm extends but there is no 'wave goodbye to the ball' action.

Follow through - moves towards the post well.

Dodging to favourite position:

Body not still at the beginning.

Body is balanced.

Weight is evenly distributed.

Feint step is too large.

Dodge step made too slow and small.

Rule infringements

Make the most of the three feet rule by keeping landing foot forward when shooting.

Make shot in three seconds.

Avoid contact when following up the shot.

Planning for improvement – Components of skill-related fitness to improve

Speed - to outmanoeuvre opponent.
Agility - manoeuvre more quickly in confined spaces.
Reaction - adjust quickly to opposition, rebounding and turn over play.
Coordination - passing and shooting accurately.

Training principles to apply

Specificity - work at performer's level and develop netball skills.

Overload - training demands put body under stress so it adapts, progresses and becomes stronger - safe levels are set for each performer.

Progression - as programme continues, individual is re-tested
- gradual changes made to frequency, intensity and time for new programme.

Practices to help improvement (isolating part of the action)

<u>Shooting</u>

1 Focus on area to improve, isolate parts of skill and gradually build back-up. Gradually increase intensity of execution.

2 Shooting practice - use check-off list with coach/observer recording and reinforcing actions.

3 Build up confidence to use skill by gradually increasing intensity of defence
   - no marker/passive marker/active marker.

<u>Dodging closer to goal</u>

1 Find optimum place for shooting by recording success rate from different places in the circle.

2 Improve ability to change direction in confined spaces whilst still maintaining balance and control:
a) in a group, use two-thirds of the court and free run into spaces, careful to avoid contact with others
b) after 30 seconds, the whistle halts run and area to run is reduced
c) repeat several times until the space is very tight - encourage players to maintain speed.

3 Apply skills to a controlled practice. Build up confidence by starting with - no marker/passive marker/active marker.

Tactics to aid improvement

Holding space so opposition is furthest position from receiving area.
Block opposition from intended direction of movement.
Players outside circle manoeuvre ball to correct place to make pass into circle.

OCR Analysis of Performance Form – Netball – Shooting

Candidate Jade Jones	Date 20/03/04	Analysis attempt First	Own/others' performance
Activity Netball - Shooting	Playing position R/handed	Experience 5 years	Conditions Dry and clear

Identified skills needed for the activity –

Balance - for a steady position on one or two feet from which to shoot.

Speed - dodging at pace to create space to receive the ball.

Coordination - combining all body actions to pass and shoot accurately.

Reaction time - ability to jump for the ball after it rebounds off the goal post.

Agility - to change direction in confined spaces to receive ball successfully in a space.

Strengths in the performance

1 Good at finding space and supporting the attacking and defensive play.

2 Successful passing in circle to goal shooter so the shot can be taken nearer the goal.

To improve strengths

1 Training principles (Finding space and supporting defence and attacking play)
Specificity

Methods Small game situation.

Practices 4 v 4 mini game:
One team attacks the goal and scores by shooting a goal (attackers). One team attacks an area in line with the centre circle (defenders). One defender and one attacker are allowed in the shooting circle.
Attackers start with the ball in the centre circle. After a goal by the attackers, the defenders restart with the ball behind the goal line. After the defenders have reached the correct area, the attackers restart from the centre circle. If the defenders are finding it too easy to score, their scoring area may be reduced.

- -

2 Training principles (Successful passing into the circle)
Specificity

Methods Drill for passing into the circle.

Practices Using two-thirds of the court and goalpost
Four players   One ball
A throws to B running into space
B throws to C running into space
C throws to D running into space

- - - - - - - - - - - - ◄ Direction of ball
◄─────── Direction of player

Weaknesses in the performance	Reasons for the weaknesses
1 Only 50% of the shots are successful.	1 Receives ball and attempts to shoot too far from goal.
2 Common fault is the shots fall short of the target.	2 The ball is held too low and to the side of the body; poor whole body action resulting in a lack of power.
3 Rebound/follow-up shot lacking.	3 Poor body position/recovery from shot and slow reactions.

How to correct the weaknesses

1 Training principles

Increase success rate of shots attempted.

Specificity   Check technique against the shooting check-off list.

Methods

Progressive practices, isolating skills required.

Performer's attempts monitored by coach/observer and results recorded.

Practices

1 Jump to receive ball, land and quickly assume correct base.
2 As above, receiving ball from different angles and heights.
3 Check correct ball support and aiming technique.
4 Combine 2 and 3.
5 Practise flexing and extending knees onto toes (without ball).
6 After legs extend, extend body and raise arms in shooting action, snapping wrist at the end.
7 Combine 5 and 6 to make stationary shot with good release position (with ball).
8 Combine all the skills together.

---

2 Training principles

(Common fault is the shots fall short of the target)

Specificity
1 Check the shooting technique is correct.
2 Shoot from prescribed places in the circle to find optimum place for successful shooting.

Methods

Experimental practice from different positions in the circle.

Practices

In the circle set out markers at six different distances and angles from the post.
Have ten shots from each position (no defence).
Score one point for every successful shot.
Repeat three times.
Keep a record of each success.
Compare the results and work out which position gives the best success.
Set a target each week increasing by 15% for three weeks.

---

3 Training principles

(Rebound/follow-up shot lacking)

Specificity

Methods

Series of progressive practices firstly using a passive and then active defence.

Practices

a) A marker stands in front of the performer in line with the post. After the shot, they have to get round the defender to get the ball.
b) A marker defends the ball for a shot but does not turn to make a rebound.
c) As above, with the marker making a moderate attempt to get the ball.
d) Full competition for marking and collection of rebounds.
e) Defender can add blocking to hinder the shooter further.

Record of discussions on findings

When the parts of the skills were understood, there was a marked improvement.

The importance of holding space prior to the feint and the dodge has now been understood.

By keeping the weight forward after the shot it gives more chance of making a successful follow-up to the shot - more work is needed on the timing of moving forward.

APPLYING KNOWLEDGE, PRINCIPLES, METHODS AND TRAINING PRACTICES

Gather as much information as you can about your sport from different sources

Applying Knowledge

Your knowledge of the event will come from different sources – personal experience, knowledge of the coaching points from teacher/coach/reference material, experience of watching peers perform and experience of watching top class performers in action on TV, video or live.

When assessing a player shooting in netball, check the following:

Are the basics right?

- Footwork
- Catching
- Throwing

Possible reasons for poor performance:

- performer does not understand the correct technique
- poor physical ability
- coordination is poor
- physical condition is not good enough
- lack of concentration
- clothing not right for the event
- the conditions may affect the performance
- tactics and strategies wrong for the situation? (Strategies are the plan – tactics are how they are put into action.)

Planning for improvement

When planning an exercise programme, the order below shows a possible train of thought that could be followed:

- identify the areas needed to improve by comparing the action with the perfect model
- isolate the part of the action needing improvement
- recognise the skill-related fitness involved
- recognise the muscles involved
- recognise the health-related factors involved

- choose the training methods that can be adapted to the event (consult the performer as there may be preferences which will make training more fun)
- test and measure the ability of the performer
- draw up your six-week plan.

Testing and measuring the skills

When testing and measuring the performer, it is important to focus on the skills and abilities needed for the particular activity. For a person to be a successful netball player in the goal attack position, the main areas needed to develop are: explosive strength (a combination of strength and speed) to spring for the ball, agility to manoeuvre into a space quickly and stamina to keep working skilfully throughout the whole game.

Tests to measure these are:

- Explosive strength – The Vertical Jump Test (see page 51)
- Stamina – The Bleep Test (see page 74)
- Agility – The Illinois Agility Test.

Agility – The Illinois Agility Test

Equipment needed:

- a large flat surface to set the course on (approximately 15m x 8m)
- eight cones (distance between cones = 3.3 metres)
- stopwatch
- recorder and recording sheet

1 The performer lies face down on the floor at the start.

2 On the whistle, the performer jumps to their feet and makes their way around the course to the finish (as in the arrows on the diagram).

3 The recorder makes a note of the total time taken from the whistle, to the performer reaching the finish.

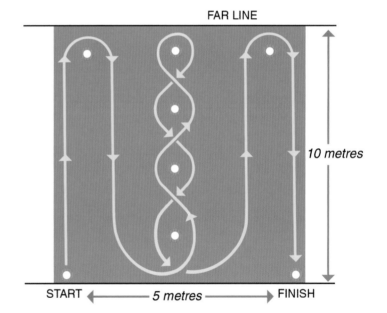

Results table for 16 year old performers					
Gender	**Excellent**	**Above average**	**Average**	**Below average**	**Poor**
Male	less than 15.9 secs	15.9–16.7 secs	16.8–17.6 secs	17.7–18.8 secs	more than 18.8 secs
Female	less than 17.5 secs	17.5–18.6 secs	18.7–22.4 secs	22.5–23.4 secs	more than 23.4 secs

Apply your knowledge of the principles of training

Principles of training to apply

Overload

To improve the performer's condition, the performer must train the body harder than usual, without risking injury. As the body becomes used to the stresses of the exercises in the programme, then the load is gradually increased. This can be done by gradually increasing some or all of the following:

- frequency
- intensity
- duration (time) spent on the exercises.

Progression

When the body becomes used to the exercise programme, changes are made to it so that further progress can be made (this is called **systematic programming**). Once the training programme is under way and regular sessions are completed each week, the body of the performer will adapt to the stress levels.

There will come a time when the original programme does not work the performer hard enough, and so has no effect. At this stage, the stresses of the programme need to be increased. The performer is tested again and changes to the programme can be made by gradually increasing the frequency, intensity and duration (time) spent on the exercise.

Specificity

When applying the principle of specificity to netball, the coach should be mindful of the following:

- the technical exercises and practices used should copy the actual movements of the body used in the game
- the exercises should be performed at the speed required in the actual match for it to be useful to the performer.

When performing the drills for improving skills such as passing, shooting or dodging, they need to be performed at a rate comparable to that used in a game situation. If they are performed too slowly in practice, the body will only be trained at that speed, and will be unable to keep up with the pace of a quick game.

Adapt the most appropriate training methods to your chosen sport

Applying training methods

Circuit training

Circuit training can target the areas of the body which need to be improved by including exercise stations solely working those areas. Circuit training is an excellent way of increasing strength and providing clearly defined challenges. This method can also bring a competitive edge to the training, as the performer knows the targets he or she has to achieve. It adds variety to the training and allows the team to work together.

The netball player can use the circuit to concentrate on the following areas: skills of the game, strength in legs, upper body and abdominal area. The performer should be tested to see what their maximum number of repetitions in the allotted time is at each station (between 20–30 seconds) and the programme based around these findings.

Below is an example of a circuit including exercises suitable for the netball player:

1 Chest passes against the wall
10 Skipping
4 Ball around the waist
2 Shuttle runs
3 Sit-ups
9 Leg raises
5 Step-ups
6 Sit up and throw
8 Agility combining footwork and throwing (stepping onto a bench alternating feet whilst chest passing the ball against a wall)
7 Shooting

▲ *A possible netball circuit.*

The circuit length can vary between six and ten stations. It is advisable to work between 20–30 seconds at each station with a 30-second rest period between each station. Complete the whole circuit, gradually building up to three to five times (sets) with a recovery period between each set of three minutes. Regular testing is necessary to measure the progress and it may be necessary to increase the intensity of the circuit. This can be done every four weeks.

Changing the numbers of stations; time of exercise; sets and repetitions can modify the intensity. The following table is an example of how the sessions can vary.

A six-week circuit training programme

Week			
1	Test and measure performer and plan the programme from findings		
	Intensity	Time at each station	Number of sets
2	65% of maximum	30 seconds	2
3	75% of maximum	20 seconds	3
4	75% of maximum	25 seconds	3
5	80% of maximum	20 seconds	2
6	Re-test and plan new programme from findings		

Interval training

This method of training works the performer at competition pace for a short burst of maximum effort and then allows a period of rest. The rest allows the body to recover and be able to repeat the effort at the highest intensity.

In netball, the performer will work all out for a short period of time (it can be as short as 15 seconds) and then recover for up to two minutes so training can continue.

Intercepting drill

This drill needs three players, one ball and two cones.

1 Two players stand opposite each other (about 4 metres apart) and consistently feed the ball to one another at the same pace.

2 The active performer continually runs between the cones, timing their run so that a successful interception can be made. If a successful interception is made the ball is passed back to one of the feeders.

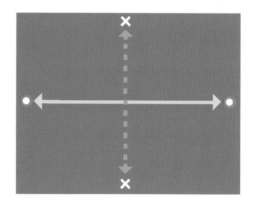

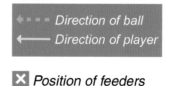
- - - Direction of ball
—— Direction of player

X Position of feeders
O Cones

3 The player works for about 20–30 seconds and then changes with one of the passing players.

This drill continues until everyone has had four attempts at being the interceptor.

▶ *A player making an interception at full stretch.*

> **Apply your knowledge of training practices to your chosen sport**

Applying training practices

When working on a personal exercise programme (**PEP**) for a performer, a good starting point is to know what the training is working towards. For instance, if the programme is for a netball player in the goal attack position, this will determine the most appropriate exercises, training methods and work rates to be applied.

▲ *Netball players at a training session.*

Testing and measuring the most important physical qualities needed (for a goal attack player – agility, endurance and power) is vital. It is from these findings that the correct level of exercise can be set. The right degree of intensity will help the performer to progress, but must not be too demanding, otherwise injury may occur.

The programme should aim to improve both health and skill-related fitness levels relevant to the particular position. So an understanding and knowledge of the event and actions involved should be taken into account and applied to the programme. This applies the principle of **specificity**.

Wherever possible an understanding of the performer's training preferences should be adapted to the programme. They may prefer working on their own, in a group, or even in a particular setting. This makes the training more interesting and enjoyable and will motivate the performer to work harder.

For the training to make a difference four sessions should be completed per week, working over 60 per cent of their maximum levels of intensity for greater than 20 minutes at a time.

Working at this frequency, intensity and duration (time), it may be that within four weeks' time, the performer's body will have adapted to the training. At this stage, a retesting of the performer is necessary, so changes can be made to the programme and further progress can be made in the future.

Timescale for a six-week PEP

The following six-week plan focuses on agility, endurance, power, general conditioning and elementary skills and techniques for the netball player. Each session starts with a warm-up and finishes with a cool down. The pattern of the programme includes interval and circuit training, technique work, skill drills and a team game, giving variety and interest for the performer.

Week 1 Test and measure: strength, stamina and speed.

Week 2 Training 1	**Week 3** Training 2
a) Technique work	a) Technique work
b) Interval training	b) Interval training
c) Circuit training	c) Circuit training
d) General game	d) General game

Week 4 Training 3	**Week 5** Training 4
a) Technique work	a) Technique work
b) Interval training	b) Interval training
c) Circuit training	c) Circuit training
d) General game	d) General game

Week 6 Re-test and measure: strength, stamina and speed. Set new programme from the findings.

Timescale of the netball year

Netball is traditionally a seasonal game played in the winter months. This factor gives shape to the training plan, together with any specific competitions and tournaments that may be scheduled. It is important to peak at the time of competition and use the periods in between to reduce the stress levels on the body so that overuse injuries do not occur.

Each part of the year plays a specific role in the development of the physical condition of the player. Some phases are highly demanding, whereas other phases specifically reduce training and allow recovery of the body.

Within the training programme, attention will be given to all aspects of the event, both physical and mental. Each session should vary in order to keep the player mentally stimulated, interested and positive. This can be achieved by mixing up technique, skill, fitness, game phases of the training and mental preparation for competition.

The netball year plan

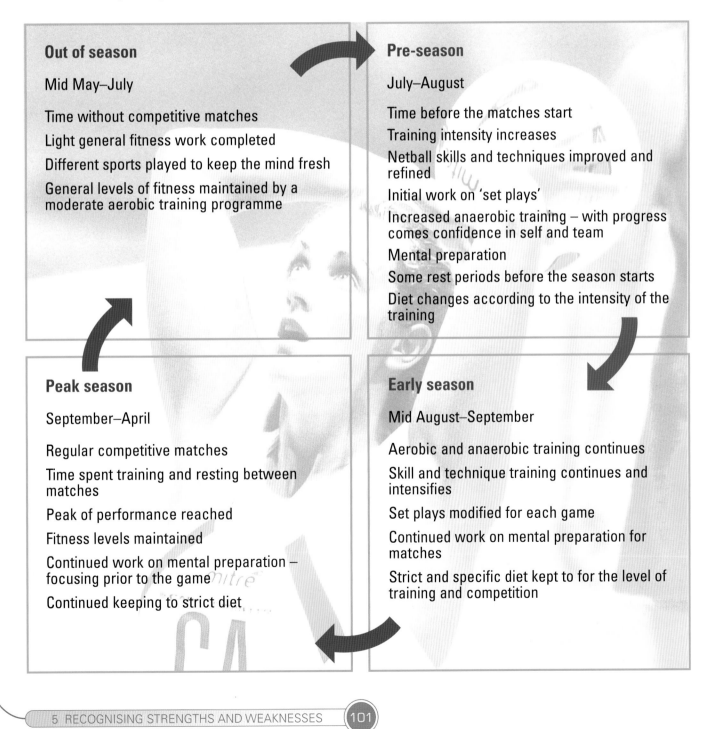

Out of season

Mid May–July

Time without competitive matches

Light general fitness work completed

Different sports played to keep the mind fresh

General levels of fitness maintained by a moderate aerobic training programme

Pre-season

July–August

Time before the matches start

Training intensity increases

Netball skills and techniques improved and refined

Initial work on 'set plays'

Increased anaerobic training – with progress comes confidence in self and team

Mental preparation

Some rest periods before the season starts

Diet changes according to the intensity of the training

Peak season

September–April

Regular competitive matches

Time spent training and resting between matches

Peak of performance reached

Fitness levels maintained

Continued work on mental preparation – focusing prior to the game

Continued keeping to strict diet

Early season

Mid August–September

Aerobic and anaerobic training continues

Skill and technique training continues and intensifies

Set plays modified for each game

Continued work on mental preparation for matches

Strict and specific diet kept to for the level of training and competition

In order to improve on a performance, participants need to know how they are performing. The coach or the observer will look and assess what they see according to their knowledge and experience of the activity. The more that is known about the activity, the more in-depth the analysis will be. Passing the results of your analysis back to a performer is called **feedback**.

Feedback can take many different forms. Some performers respond best to a particular style of feedback. The coach should recognise these preferences and choose the most suitable form for the individual. The type of information to be given as feedback may also suit a particular style.

The timing of feedback is often crucial. A player may have had a bad training session or match and is angry or upset, so giving the feedback straightaway may not be productive. The relationship between the coach and the performer may also have a bearing on the type of feedback given.

Positive feedback

Positive feedback is good at motivating performers. It tells them what is good about their performance so that they can refer to this in future performances and repeat the good aspects of the action.

Negative feedback

This type of feedback tells the performer what is incorrect about the performance. Too much of this kind of feedback can damage the confidence of a performer. A good way of using this type of feedback is to give it after some positive feedback.

Intrinsic feedback

Intrinsic feedback originates from within the performer in response to their own movement. All sports people are able to feel or sense how well they are performing.

Extrinsic feedback

This is any information gathered from sources other than the movement produced in the action. It will aim to complement intrinsic feedback by highlighting:

- knowledge of the performance – provided by the coach or from watching a video giving information about the technique and performance. This could be an analysis of a penalty kick action for example
- knowledge of the results – information given to do with the result of the performance. An example of this could be relating the number of successful shots scored by a basketball player, after looking at the statistics.

FOOTBALL PERFORMANCE SHEET

Candidate	Position	Conditions	Date

OUTFIELD PLAYER *(Tick or cross depending on success)*		GOALKEEPER *(Tick or cross depending on success)*	
PASSING –		**SHOTS SAVED –**	
Short		One-handed to left	
Medium		One-handed to right	
Long		Two-handed to left	
Shot on Goal		Two-handed to right	
Header		**CONTROL –**	
Throw in		High Catch	
BALL CONTROL –		**CLEARANCES –**	
1 Touch		One-handed Punch	
2 Touches		Two-handed Punch	
Dribbling		Kick	
Chesting Down		Header	
Control on Thigh			
GENERAL –		**PASSES –**	
Tackles		Underarm	
Fouls		Overarm	

▲ *An analysis designed for football.*

The timing of giving feedback has different effects on the performer:

Before training

Prepares the performer and focuses their mind on the job in hand. Also allows the performer to be reflective of previous performances.

During training

Pinpoints the area to concentrate on at the precise moment it happens. This makes the part to focus on clear and allows changes to be made during the session.

Immediately after training

Highlights successes and failures in the game whilst they are still clear in everyone's mind. The performer and the coach, however, may be tired and emotionally drained so sometimes only a general response to the training is made at this time.

The day after training

Waiting until the next day to talk to the player/performer usually leads to a calmer environment. The delivery of the feedback is likely to be better thought through, as the coach will have consulted the performance records, times, distances etc. (extrinsic feedback). Changes may already have been made to the training sessions as a result. The time between the event and the feedback makes the performer more reflective about a match or event, as there will have been time for their intrinsic reactions to be logically thought about, and therefore they can be added to any discussions.

Before a competition or match

Prepares the performer for the task in hand and aims to focus the mind on the event or opposition. It can also be a chance to 'psyche up' the team and motivate them for the event.

During the competition or match

The amount of feedback that can be given depends on the sport. In athletics, for example, it is against the rules for the coach to give instructions to the athlete from inside the track.

▼ *A basketball coach giving feedback during a time-out.*

Analysis of Performance for GCSE PE

A lot of coaches are present but they are outside the track and can only communicate from there. In team games, managers and coaches can often be seen giving instructions. In football, there is a technical area in which the manager is compelled to stay; when they don't they can be given yellow and red cards in the same way that players can. Some activities like basketball incorporate the need to give feedback during the game by having time-out rules.

Immediately after the match

This type of feedback can be emotional as those concerned may be elated or devastated depending on the outcome of the performance. The players are tired at this time, so usually only a general response to the overall performance is given with little reference to analysis.

The day after the match or competition

This is a more measured way of giving feedback. All parties are calm and have had the chance to think about what to say. The coach may well have taken the opportunity to look at the performance results and statistics and be able to make use of them during the feedback session.

▼ *Out of season training includes a general training programme.*

2 ▶ SETTING TARGETS

When setting targets, the starting point for the coach and performer is to think about what goals they are aiming for. It is from here that all targets and decisions will follow.

Long-term planning

Long-term planning takes into account an athlete's ability to progress and aims at a given standard, event or competition in the future. For athletes, this may be a four-year plan leading up to the next Olympics.

Seasonal programme

Out of season, light general fitness is undertaken – different sports can be undertaken to keep the mind fresh. A performer's general level of fitness is maintained by a moderate **aerobic** training programme.

Pre-season

Before the match or competition, training intensity increases and skills and techniques are improved and refined. More **anaerobic** training is usually undertaken.

Early season

Aerobic and anaerobic training continues, as well as skill training. Mental preparation and some rest are undertaken before competitions.

Peak season

During peak season competitions are more frequent. The performer's time is spent training and resting between competitions. Training should aim to have the athlete at peak performance level for each competition or fixture. Work on mental preparation, diet and appropriate exercise is undertaken leading up to the event.

Specific planning

When devising a personal training programme **systematic training** takes into account the individual needs of the performer. Prior to training, the performer is tested and measured to find out the strength and capabilities of the heart, lungs and muscle groups. From the findings, the degree of difficulty of the training sessions can be set.

As the training sessions are regularly completed, the body adapts to the stresses of the exercise. The performer is re-tested and measured in the same way and from the findings changes are made to the sessions. The result will be that the frequency, intensity, time and type of exercises will change so the performer can make further progress. The results of each training session and the different programmes provide a reference point, along with evidence of the progress made.

Different targets

There are different types of targets in sport and different ways to set them. They can be put under the headings of short-, medium- and long-term goals. Each sport has its own targets and when carefully and realistically set they can motivate individuals to improve their performance.

Short-term targets

These are everyday goals to work towards. They occur within the training programme itself and help the performer to focus on working hard. By working hard on the programme, the body adapts, so a new programme needs to be set so that further progress can be made. By adapting the session and setting individual targets within it, the performer's interest is kept and is hopefully motivated by the changes.

The following list identifies some different ways to set targets in a training session:

- beat own target set in a previous session
- beat the score of a partner who is of a similar ability
- attain a percentage of the maximum score available (from personal information collected in previous sessions – e.g. perform 80 per cent of the maximum number of sit-ups capable of)
- reach a stated level
- increase the lifts in a weight training session by a small percentage
- increase the time spent on an activity for a session.

Short-term targets for you	
1	Complete all coursework.
2	Complete homework.
3	Learn new information.
4	Practise skills to get them right.
5	Work hard in the lessons.

Mid-term targets

As the body adapts to a training programme, it is important to increase the amount of work done in each session for further progress to be made. The performer is re-tested and measured so that the intensity of the exercises can be changed to fit more accurately the new capabilities of the body. Working through a new training programme, therefore, could be classed as a mid-term target.

Within a season, an athlete may aim their sights at reaching a new level of performance. Months of work may go into improving times or distances in time for an event. In team games, a mid-term goal may be to be in the top five of a league by a certain time, like December for instance.

Mid-term targets for you	
1	Keep all information from lessons safe.
2	Refer to past work when necessary.
3	Work towards completing analysis/PEP.
4	Practise analysing performance.
5	Revise for mock examinations.
6	Respond to marks and comments for practical and written work.
7	Improve your marks/percentages by a certain level and time.
8	Improve and maintain personal fitness levels.

Long-term targets

A team may set its sights on a particular competition or winning a league for the season. A top class athlete may have a four-year plan to qualify for the Olympic Games. All the work they do in the meantime, in training and competitions, works towards that final, ultimate target.

Long-term targets for you	
1	Complete all coursework and keep it in order, so that it is easy to revise from.
2	Have a bank of analysis documentation readily available for the examiner.
3	Revise all work fully.
4	Practise practical activities and develop to a high standard.
5	Practise analysis of performance several times.
6	Aim to achieve a certain grade.

3 ▶ MONITORING

There may be times during the course when you have to monitor a performance as a candidate, a coach or a performer. Checking your own work and performance will be an ongoing process but you will also have to assess the effectiveness of a training programme.

In order to monitor successfully, a careful watch must be made on the performance and together with knowledge, advice and experience, minor or major changes for the performer can be made.

When monitoring the training programme check that it is following the SPORT route:

S – Specificity

P – Progression

O – Overload

R – Reversibility

T – Tedium

Keeping to these main guides will ensure that the programme fits with the sport and is set at the level which enables suitable progress to be made, develops an understanding of the need for regular exercise to maintain fitness levels and the need to make the sessions interesting.

When monitoring a performance or training programme, it is be necessary to make sure that:

- the session is carried out safely
- each part of the programme content is performed
- the correct amount of training is completed
- the results are recorded.

▶ *A personal trainer or coach closely monitors the effects of performance on the individual.*

4 EVALUATING

Evaluation is the process of weighing up a performance and making the necessary changes for improvement after observation, analysis and discussion.

There are several stages to this process:

- decide what to measure (skills/strength etc.)
- choose a way of measuring
- record and keep the results
- analyse the results
- decide on a course of action
- put the decisions into action.

One way of evaluating a performance is to use a performance result sheet. This method uses a form containing the skills of the activity. Each time a skill is observed, it is noted down. By using skill sheets in a game or practice session, evidence will build up of the effectiveness of the performer.

Studying the results will show not only the best and worst areas of the performance, but also those areas in need of fine-tuning only. Consequently, decisions can be made and applied to a new programme with different targets.

5 UNDERSTANDING LEADERSHIP (EDEXCEL)

Although all the leaders linked with a sports team have an influence on the team, most of the time there are instances when one particular person makes the greatest impression. In preparing for the game, the coach devises the training and will have the most influence; before the game, the manager will give final instructions and attempt to motivate the players; and within the game, the captain will influence play on the pitch. In rugby, where there are distinct divisions of play requiring different skills and mind sets, there may well be a leader of the backs and one for the forwards on the field of play.

Each person in a leadership role will influence others in a different way:

Captain

- Performs formalities – tosses for ends, introduces players, carries out diplomatic duties.
- Influences the team both on and off the pitch.
- Leads by example.
- Controls the players.
- Calls for particular type of strategies to be employed.
- Motivates the players.
- Encourages others to overcome difficulties.
- Calms players down in heated situations.
- Gives new instructions to the players.
- Keeps the team playing as a unit and working hard.
- Mediates between management and players on and off the pitch.

▲ *Patrick Vieira*

Manager

- Selects the team.
- Puts the right blend of personalities and skills in the team for greatest success.
- Liaises with coach about form of the players.
- Praises and criticises play.
- Supports the players publicly.
- Disciplines the players when necessary.
- Buys new players.
- Sells players.
- Deals with publicity.
- Mediates between the chairperson and the coach.

▲ *Arsene Wenger*

Coach

- Monitors the progress and form of the players.
- Knows the players and sets achievable goals to suit their abilities and personalities.
- Devises the training sessions for individual players.
- Organises the content of the training sessions for the team.
- Makes training interesting, fun and challenging.
- Divides the training for the different players (e.g. goalkeeping coaching).

▲ *Pat Rice*

- Sets targets for the team to achieve.
- Organises the equipment for the training session.
- Evaluates players' performances.
- Motivates the players.
- Rewards good work when appropriate.
- Organises players' diets.
- Mediates between manager and players.

Style of management

Anyone in an influential position will adopt a different style according to his or her experience, confidence and personality. There is no ideal style of leadership. Good leadership depends on how well you adapt the role to your personality, which will be reflected in the level of performance of the people you are leading and the confidence they have in you in this role.

Some leaders will:
- control everything and so become the driving force
- accommodate others as their prime care is to the people concerned
- think logically and work through a problem, often coming across as being blunt and forceful.

Comparison of the managerial styles of Sir Alex Ferguson and Sven-Goran Eriksson

Although both men are football managers, they have completely different jobs. Ferguson has total control over his players and continual contact with them on a daily basis, whereas Eriksson sees his players only intermittently and is dependent on the clubs to look after the players' well-being. Both men have had their jobs for different lengths of time, but nonetheless both Ferguson and Eriksson have managed to bring great levels of success to their teams. Both men are highly respected for the job they are doing.

Forthright • Confrontational
• Animated • Emotional
• Thoughtful about the game
• Severe in criticism
• Outbursts of anger
• Single-minded
• Speaks his mind seemingly without reservation

Quiet man • Self-controlled
• Motivator
• Respectful of the players
• Thoughtful about the game
• Quietly critical of performance
• Instils confidence in players
• Good man manager
• Open to ideas

6 ▶ DIFFERENT ROLES IN THE ACTIVITY (SPECIFICALLY FOR AQA)

Many team sports or activities often have different requirements of the performers within the structure of the squad. Players in the same team may need to acquire different skills to the others, so they can add to the overall successful play of the team. As a result, the necessary skill-related components will differ according to their position on the field of play.

The most obvious changes in skill requirement are between outfield players and goalkeepers. In this example, for instance, both players will need agility, but the outfield player needs this component of skill in order to work his way around the opposition travelling with the ball; the goalkeeper, however, needs agility to change direction and make a save in a single action. Therefore the training for both types of player will have specific differences. Although the example given is the most obvious one, there are many differences in each outfield player's skills too.

Netball example

Netball is played with tight controls on the players' movements about the court. Each player has a specific job to play in the team. They have a varied amount of court to cover and are expected to play either a defensive or attacking role. As a result of these precise responsibilities, the physical characteristics of each player are distinct.

In general, the players who are allowed in the circle will be the tallest so that they can shoot and defend the high ball, whereas the centre, who is required to run fast and change direction quickly, will need a low centre of gravity, and will therefore be shorter. The different positions also require different qualities from the players. Some players will need to concentrate throughout the match as their involvement is continual, others may have periods of the game when they are not in action, but will still have to be focused on the game, although from a distance.

In general, the following can be said about a netball team:

Goal Keeper

- Often the tallest player
- Stops the goal shooter scoring – able to stretch and reach to defend a shot
- Can jump high so has good explosive leg strength (mobile in a confined space)
- Continually concentrates on her opponent player – good anaerobic respiration.

Goal Defence

- Has good reactions to intercept passes to the shooters
- Is tall to stop the goal attack shooting
- Able to stretch and reach to defend a shot – can jump high so has good explosive leg strength
- Good mobility in order to take the ball out of attack
- Good aerobic and anaerobic respiration.

Wing Defence

- Is of moderate height
- Good mobility in defensive goal and centre thirds
- Helps take the ball from the defence to the attack
- Has speed of movement and agility
- Good aerobic and anaerobic respiration.

Centre

- Usually the shortest player
- Quickest player linking defence with attack – very agile
- Has good reactions – can defend and attack – quick to see the play change and adapt their role in the game
- Excellent aerobic and anaerobic respiration.

Wing Attack

- Is of moderate height
- Good mobility in the attacking goal and centre thirds
- Helps take the ball into the attack and supports the goal attack and shooter around the circle
- Has speed of movement and agility
- Good aerobic and anaerobic respiration.

Goal Attack

- Is tall to help with shooting
- Can jump high so has good explosive leg strength
- Accurate with shooting and throwing – good hand-eye coordination
- Very mobile to help get the ball into the attacking circle
- Good aerobic and anaerobic respiration.

▲ *The England netball team comprises players of different heights.*

Goal Shooter

- Usually one of the tallest players
- Accurate with passing and especially shooting (good hand-eye coordination)
- Can jump high, so has good explosive leg strength (mobile in a confined space)
- Has good anaerobic respiration.

Football example

All players should have both aerobic and anaerobic capacity. Depending on the position they play in, the type of respiration used will vary to different degrees – a goalkeeper relies on short bursts of movement (anaerobic), whereas a midfielder needs to be moving on the pitch continually (aerobic).

The basic skills are similar for all players, but certain positions require a specialised way of putting the skills into action. For instance, a defender will generally tackle in a completely different way to a forward. If a player has a dominant kicking foot then this may determine which side of the field they play on. A player who naturally kicks with their left foot will be best placed on the left-hand side of the pitch so that they can cross the ball into the 18 yard box more efficiently.

The main groupings of the players (apart from the goalkeeper) are defenders, midfielders and forwards. The jobs of the players vary depending on the tactics employed by the team. The following descriptions of players' roles in the team are based on the 4–4–2 system of play.

Goalkeeper

- Identified player to use hands
- Last line of defence
- Agile and strong
- Keen reactions
- Usually tall
- Strong dead-ball kick
- Good anaerobic capacity.

DEFENDERS

Together they will keep the line for the offside trap, aim to dominate the last third of the pitch, protect the 18 yard box and help take the ball from the defence to the attack.

▲ *Goalkeeper: David James*

Left back

- Good anaerobic capacity for reacting to opposition
- Physically strong
- Left-footed kicker
- Strong tackler
- Good medium and long passer
- Able to close mark a player in the 18 yard box without fouling.

Centre backs (x 2)

- Usually tall
- Physically imposing
- Good anaerobic capacity for reacting to opposition
- Excellent tacklers
- Good medium and long passers
- Able to close mark a player in the 18 yard box without fouling
- Excellent headers of the ball.

Right back

- Good anaerobic capacity for reacting to opposition
- Physically strong
- Right-footed kicker
- Strong tackler
- Good medium and long passer
- Able to close mark a player in the 18 yard box without fouling.

MIDFIELDERS

They aim to dominate the middle third of the pitch and link the defence with the attack.

Left midfield

- Excellent aerobic and anaerobic capacity
- Can track players back
- Good timing in the tackle
- Left-footed kicker
- Reads the game well
- Excellent long pass skills for crosses.

▲ *Left back: Roberto Carlos*

▲ *Left midfielder: Ryan Giggs*

Centre midfield (x 2)

- Excellent aerobic and anaerobic capacity
- Can track back players
- Good timing in the tackle
- Reads the game well
- Excellent passing skills.

Right midfield

- Excellent aerobic and anaerobic capacity
- Can track players back
- Good timing in the tackle
- Right-footed kicker
- Reads the game well
- Excellent long pass skills for crosses.

▲ *Right midfielder: David Beckham*

FORWARDS

They aim to take on the opposition's defence and attack the 18 yard box. Often one forward is quick and agile and the other one is strong and imposing.

Forward

- Excellent anaerobic capacity
- Agile
- Excellent dribbling skills
- Reads the game well
- Excellent speed off the spot.

Forward

- Excellent anaerobic capacity
- Strong
- Good in the air
- Physically imposing.

▲ *Forward: Ronaldo*

7 DISCUSSING FINDINGS WITH THE PERFORMER

After studying a person's performance, an interactive discussion with the performer should follow. This will give them a chance to understand the comments made about their performance and give their views on the analysis. This is the feedback process and will work on two levels:

- how useful the feedback was to the performer
- a reaction to your skills as an analyst.

The questions you ask should be easy to understand, relevant to the activity and will make the performer think about their effectiveness in the activity.

The aspects of feedback

Who?

The skills needed to give feedback seem simple, but can be difficult depending on the performer and performance. The person receiving the feedback will want to be treated with respect, irrespective of their skill level, and have appropriate comments made. Not only is it important to have the ability to comment on positive and negative aspects of the action, but it is equally important to be able to discuss how each aspect can be developed and improved. This leaves the performer with a positive target for the future.

It is important to make a record of a feedback session. To make the process run smoothly, you must be able to write the responses down quickly and clearly. There may be times when you need to be able to ask the same question in a variety of ways. A particular question may simply stump the performer. Be prepared by practising this skill regularly. Always keep focused on the action seen and ask appropriate questions about it. Writing a series of questions down and asking them from a list will help.

Where?

Deciding on the place to give feedback depends on the environmental conditions. If the activity has taken place outside, then the weather may be a deciding factor, as it may be windy, wet and cold. It may also be awkward to write responses legibly outdoors. Other activities may still be in progress so there may be distractions from the questioning. An immediate response will net some fresh ideas; however, the performer may be getting cold and may be tired after the activity, so answers may be unclear.

The feedback could take place in a quiet classroom, providing a business-like environment with no distractions, which should lend itself to a better quality of responses.

When?

This will depend on the activity, conditions, individual and the time available. If outdoors, poor conditions may make it impractical to go for an immediate response. Not only will the conditions be unfavourable but also the tiredness of the individual may have a negative bearing on the quality of responses too.

To get a more measured response, there could be time given for the performer to change after the activity and a quiet, comfortable classroom used in which to conduct the feedback. The time gap will give the performer an opportunity to settle their thoughts, possibly leading to more reflective answers.

Why?

The reasons for the feedback process should be made clear to the individual. Ultimately the feedback will aim to improve understanding of strengths and weaknesses in the performance and it should be used to modify future training. By conducting a question and answer session, the performer will become reflective about their performance and possibly think more about their training and competition results in the future.

The way you conduct the feedback session will earn you marks in the examination.

What?

Have a clear idea of what you want to achieve from the discussion. The questions should concentrate on the performance in hand. A series of questions could ask for a response on the person's present level of ability, what their strengths and weaknesses are, how they can improve and to what levels they should aim in the future.

Some questioning can be about how the analysis was conducted and whether the responses were clearly given.

How?

How the process is set up and executed can have an effect on the quality of the responses. Set aside ample time for the feedback to be given, so that the performer does not feel rushed and can put more thought into their answers. If it is rushed, the process is undervalued and loses its importance.

Any instructions that will help the smooth running of the feedback should be given prior to the session. The language used should be appropriate to the ability of the individual. A quiet environment will help the individual to concentrate on the questions.

Ways of recording reactions and views

There are many ways of recording information, so it is best to choose the method most suitable for you, the activity and the performer. The record of the feedback sessions will form part of your coursework, so keep it safe and in order. If there is anything left outstanding, complete it in good time.

Using questions and answers

Question and answer sessions are similar to questionnaires, but verbal questions and responses are given and recorded. It can add a personal touch to the process, but it can be difficult to hand-write the responses quickly, and taking time to keep your handwriting legible may make the procedure boring. Using this method, however, gives the opportunity for the interviewer to further explain a point if the question is found to be difficult. One way of overcoming this is to tape the session, though you will need to ask the performer's permission. Answers can be written out later at your convenience.

Examples of possible questions that can be used:

About the personal exercise programme:

- Were you tested before the programme started?
- Did the programme make you work hard?
- Was the programme easy to complete?
- Was the programme varied enough to keep your interest?
- Did you get feedback after each session?
- Before you were tested did you think that you were stronger than you actually were?
- Which part of the programme was your favourite?
- How were you motivated throughout the programme? (self/coach/teacher/friends)
- Did you need motivating in the programme?
- What surprised you about the re-testing after the programme was finished?

About the individual's performance:

- How do you think you performed?
- What were your strengths?
- What were your weaknesses?
- Which areas of skill-related fitness did you think you mostly used?
- Did you think you put your training into operation?
- How did you put your training into operation?

- How do you think the training should change as the result of your performance?
- What area of skills will you work on as a result of this performance?
- Were you happy with your passing, for example, in the game?
- What targets will you set yourself for the future?
- How accurate do you think your skills were in the performance?
- Did the conditions affect your performance at all?
- How good do you think your performance was?

About the team performance:

- What did you contribute to the team performance?
- How did you contribute to the team performance?
- Which area of the pitch were you the most effective in?
- How did your side/area of the team (as a small unit) perform?
- Were the opposition a good match for your team?
- Were members of the team supportive to one another?
- Did the behaviour and reactions of members of the team have an influence on the team's performance?

Written report

A written report takes the form of a small essay. This is time-consuming to produce and can be long-winded to read. It relies on the ability of the reporter to be able to write logically and coherently.

Notes

Notes contain short, relevant pointers about the subject. These get straight to the point and can be easier to follow than the full written account. They can direct a person more easily to a main point of interest. There is a skill to writing good notes; if they are too brief then they miss the point. Notes are easier and quicker to read than a full report.

Check-off list

The relevant techniques for an activity are broken down and set out as a list. To the side of each statement, there is a box that can be ticked if the relevant skill is identified in the performance. The results are easy to see with this method. There can only be a positive or negative response to the performance, so even though the performer may just have missed the correct technique, it still receives a negative response. An accompanying discussion with the performer may be needed to give more feedback of the performance to support this method.

CHECK-OFF LIST FOR ATHLETICS – SHOT PUT		Tick if successful
GRIP	Shot at base of three, outspread fingers with thumb and little finger supporting	
STANCE	Shot in contact with the neck and elbow high.	
CROUCH	Facing the back of the circle	
	Weight on right leg	
	Body low and closed	
	Left knee in close to the right.	
SHIFT	Lean body towards the toe board	
	Drive back on right leg whilst extending left leg vigorously	
	Keeping body low	
	Rotate the hips outwards so at right angles with the closed shoulders.	
PUT POSITION	Weight transfers from back to front leg	
	Fast right pushing hips to the front	
	Right leg extends (causing the lift).	
LIFT	Left arm swings down and back	
	Right shoulder driven outwards.	
STRIKE	When shoulders square – with elbow high	
	Arm punches the shot out at the last moment as a result of the leg and hip action	
	Left shoulder kept high too.	
RELEASE	Approximately 40 degrees (elite athletes release between 30–40 degrees)	
	With elbow high and in line with the shot	
	Arm punches forward	
	Wrist flips so thumb pointing downwards.	
RECOVERY	Once shot released right leg moves to the front to stop forward motion.	

Performance sheet

The stated skills needed for successful play are set out in a matrix. Every time the skill is performed a mark is made at the relevant point. This will show how many times the skills are performed in the game and may show areas to improve. Training or an explanation should be given on how to read the information and what each response means – is it a negative or positive?

NETBALL PERFORMANCE SHEET			
Candidate	**Assessed position**	**Playing conditions**	**Date**
SKILLS (Tick or cross depending on success)		**INFRINGEMENT** (Tick or cross depending on success)	
PASSING –		**CONTACT –**	
Chest		Obstruction	
Javelin		Footwork	
Bounce		Offside	
Two-handed overhead		Replayed ball	
Throw on		Held ball	
DEFENDING –		Over a third	
Interception		**SHOOTING** (*Put a cross in position of shot*) Record the number of successful shots for each area	
Blocking			
GENERAL –		NEAR /	
Toss up			
		MID /	
		FAR /	

Questionnaire

A questionnaire relies on the ability of the person answering to read the questions properly and write down their responses clearly. The language has to be appropriate to the level of the ability of the performer. Clear instructions on how to fill in the questionnaire should be given prior to completion. This will familiarise the person with the language and what kind of response a question is expecting. When devising a feedback sheet using this method, group the questions together by subject and put them in a logical sequence. There are several ways a questionnaire can be used. Choose the one most appropriate to your needs:

a) It can be taken away and filled in without a time limit. The problem with this method is that if a question is found to be difficult to answer it is left blank. Questionnaires can also become lost and it can be difficult to collect them back in.

b) The question can be read out to the person, they make their response and the interviewer writes it down. This may be easy to assess later.

c) The person sits on their own and fills in the questionnaire and can ask for help if necessary.

NAME	FORM	DATE

ACTIVITY

Please answer the questions in the spaces provided

PERSONAL ABILITY

1 What do you think is your main strength in the activity?

_____

2 What do you think is your main weakness in the activity?

_____

3 In the activity, which skill did you find the most difficult to perform?

_____

TRAINING PROGRAMME

4 Did the training programme devised for you suit your ability?

_____

5 What personal qualities did it take to complete the training programme?

_____

6 Are there any changes, from your experience, you would make to a future training programme?

Five-point scale

This method poses specific questions and asks for a response by ticking an appropriate box. There are usually up to five boxes available, ranging from the least desirable response to the best. The person makes their choice based on their experience.

The following factors need to be taken into consideration when using this method:

- give clear instructions on how to fill in the sheet
- make the level of each box clear so that the correct response can be made
- use language appropriate to the ability of the user
- make the questions relevant to the experience of the performer
- group the questions together and put them in a logical order to help the user.

Like the questionnaire sheet it can be:

a) taken away and filled in without a time limit

b) read out to the person; they make their response and the interviewer writes it down

c) filled in privately; the person can ask for help if necessary.

8 ▸ KEEPING RECORDS

Every piece of work you complete is important, even if it is not as good as you hoped it would be. Each piece will tell you what is successful and unsuccessful about your efforts. Learning to repeat the good areas and apply them to other situations and put the bad points right are all part of the process to success.

Keep your student's file in order and up to date. Try to make every piece as legible as you can, as this will be the document you will revise from the most. Bring it to each lesson, despite the fact that it can get worn and be cumbersome. If your file is with you, new work can easily be put in the right place and not be mislaid. Apart from coursework from the theory lesson, other items for safe keeping may include:

- past examination papers with results
- analysis attempts (for a performer and official)
- records of personal practical work
- information about the examination requirements.

Information can be kept on disk, but as there may not be access to a computer during lesson time, this should be kept as a back-up to your file.

The advantages of using a disk are:

- it is easy to carry
- information can easily be modified
- templates can easily be logged in and worked on
- typing is often neater than handwriting so is easier to revise from
- by using the spellcheck many spelling mistakes can be eliminated.

The disadvantages of using a disk are:

- you need access to a computer
- they are easy to mislay.

CONCLUSION

To achieve the best results for this part of the course, all the aspects must be given serious consideration. Take every opportunity to practise refereeing or umpiring, for instance. If you have never umpired, start with small game situations and choose the infringements you will pick up on. Go out of your way to learn the correct terminology of your chosen activity. As you become more experienced, using the correct technical terms will become second nature. Good use of the terminology will show the examiner the expertise you have developed.

When observing, always have in mind the perfect model. Whichever activity you choose, always try to watch a match or competition with the top competitors in action. Record top class events from the television and practise your analysis skills by freeze-framing the video and looking at technique. This will build up your idea of what a good performance consists of when observing and analysing for your exam.

Keep records of your observations and evaluations. These will provide evidence of the work you have covered. When giving feedback, make sure your comments are clear and constructive, starting with the good points first. Always plan your work – know what you have to do to complete the work well and plan your strategy weekly to achieve the best results.

Good luck!

GLOSSARY

A

Aerobic   'with oxygen'; when exercise is moderate and steady, the heart can supply all the oxygen the working muscles need

Agility   the ability to change the position of the body quickly and to control the movement of the whole body easily

Anaerobic   'without oxygen'; when exercising in short, fast bursts, the heart cannot supply blood and oxygen to the muscles as fast as the cells can use them, so energy is released without oxygen present

Analysis   a study or examination breaking down the subject into parts

B

Balance   the ability to retain the centre of mass (gravity) of the body above the base of support with reference to static (stationary) or dynamic (changing) conditions of movement, shape and orientation

Bleep Test   (multi-stage fitness test) a running test measuring heart and lung efficiency

Body composition   the proportion of body weight that is fat, muscle and bone, normally measured as a percentage

C

Captain   designated leader of a group/team

Check-off list   a form containing a detailed list of components ticked off when identified

Circuit training   a series of exercises completed in order and for a certain time limit

Closed skill   an action performed with no external interference

Coach   person who instructs others in ways to improve

Communication   two or more parties relaying information between each other

Cool down   exercises after the main activity, gradually bringing the body systems back to near resting state

Coordination   the ability to perform complex moves using two or more body parts together

D

DOMS   (delayed onset muscle soreness) possible consequence of a failure to complete a thorough cool down after exercise

Dynamic stretching   the athlete moves into the stretch position and 'bounces' the muscle

E

Endurance   the ability to keep working over a period of time without tiring or losing skill

Evaluation   after studying an action or data calculating its effectiveness

Exercise   a form of physical activity done primarily to improve one's health and physical fitness

F

Fartlek training   'speed play': changing speed, distances and times of exercise, with rests in the same session

Feedback   related information given about a subject

Fitness   ability to meet the demands of the environment

Five-point scale   a form containing points for observation requiring a graded response

Flexibility   joints' ability to move to their full range

G

Governing body   a group responsible for the rules, procedures and fixtures of a particular game or event

H

Health   a state of complete social, mental and physical well-being

Health-related fitness   the effectiveness of a person's cardiovascular system, flexibility, muscular endurance, muscular strength and body composition to meet the demands of the environment

Heart rate   the number of times the heart beats per minute

I

Illinois Agility Test   a running test measuring the agility of a performer

Infringement   action in a game that breaks the rules

Interval training   mixing periods of hard exercise with rest periods

M

Manager   person in charge who organises and makes decisions influencing others

Minimum level of fitness   the resulting fitness level when over a period of weeks three to five exercise sessions of 20 minutes, raising the heart rate to 60–80% of its maximum, are completed

Movement   in motion, could be an action like running or swinging a racket at a ball

Muscular strength   the amount of force a muscle can exert against a resistance in one attempt

N

Non verbal terminology a series of specialised signals peculiar to an activity

O

Objective analysis   study of a performance relying on statistics

Observation   a visual study of a subject

Officiate   to have a specific and decisive job in an event ensuring the rules are kept

Open skill   an action performed adapting to external influences

Overload   following the principle that the body can only be improved through training more and harder then normal

P

Perfect model   what is technically regarded as the best way to perform a sporting action

Performance   how well a task is completed

Personal exercise programme (PEP)   training designed specifically for one individual

Power   the ability to complete strength performances quickly; power = strength x speed

Progression   starting slowly and gradually increasing the amount of exercise completed

Pyramid sets   a system where the performer starts with the easiest weights, gradually and systematically increasing the intensity of the load but with fewer repetitions

Q

Questionnaire   a series of questions about a subject requiring a written response

R

Reaction time   the time between the presentation of a stimulus and the onset of a movement

Referee   person in charge of a game who controls, makes decisions and ensures fair play between parties

Regularity   repeating exercise sessions in a week to bring about improved fitness

Reversibility   any adaptation that takes place as a consequence of training will be reversed when a person stops training

Rules   a set of previously decided conventions to abide by

S

Simple sets   the same weight is lifted a prescribed number of repetitions and sets

Skill-related fitness   physical motor abilities of the body adapted to specific sports

Specificity   concentrating on specific kinds of activity or exercise to build specific body parts

Speed   the differential rate at which an individual is able to perform a movement or cover a distance in a period of time

Stamina   the ability to keep working at a moderate to hard level over long periods

Static stretching   muscles are flexed without further movement and held for about ten seconds

Strategy   a plan designed to lead to success

Subjective analysis   study of a performance relying on emotion and opinion

Systematic training   planning a programme for an individual as a result of the effect of previous training

T

Tactics   the specific ways and methods implemented to lead to success

Technical term   words used that are peculiar to that subject/activity alone

Terminology   language and vocabulary

Time-lapsed photography   a series of pictures taken momentarily after each other

Training   a planned programme which uses scientific principles to improve performance, skill, game ability and motor and physical fitness

Training methods   a way of training that works a particular part of the body in a certain way

Training principles   ideas behind the effects of training

V

Verbal terminology   a series of specialised words peculiar to an activity relayed by speech

VO_2 max   maximum amount of oxygen the body can take in

W

Warm-up   exercises gradually putting stresses on the body systems in preparation for the main activity

Weight training   progressively lifting heavier weights to improve strength or lifting weights more often to improve stamina

Written report   a written account of a particular subject